California Mission Architecture

A Survey and Sourcebook

Jock M. Sewall, A.I.A.

Other Schiffer Books by the Author:

Mediterranean Architecture: A Sourcebook of Architectural Elements, 978-0-7643-3891-5, $100.00

Library of Congress Control Number: 2012949673

Type set in Minion Pro

ISBN: 978-0-7643-4200-4
Printed in Hong Kong

Published by Schiffer Publishing, Ltd.
4880 Lower Valley Road
Atglen, PA 19310
Phone: (610) 593-1777; Fax: (610) 593-2002
E-mail: Info@schifferbooks.com

In Europe, Schiffer books are distributed by
Bushwood Books
6 Marksbury Ave.
Kew Gardens
Surrey TW9 4JF England
Phone: 44 (0) 20 8392 8585; Fax: 44 (0) 20 8392 9876
E-mail: info@bushwoodbooks.co.uk
Website: www.bushwoodbooks.co.uk

California Mission Architectu

A Survey and Sourcebook

Schiffer Publishing Ltd
880 Lower Valley Road • Atglen, PA 19310

Jock M. Sewall, A.I.A.

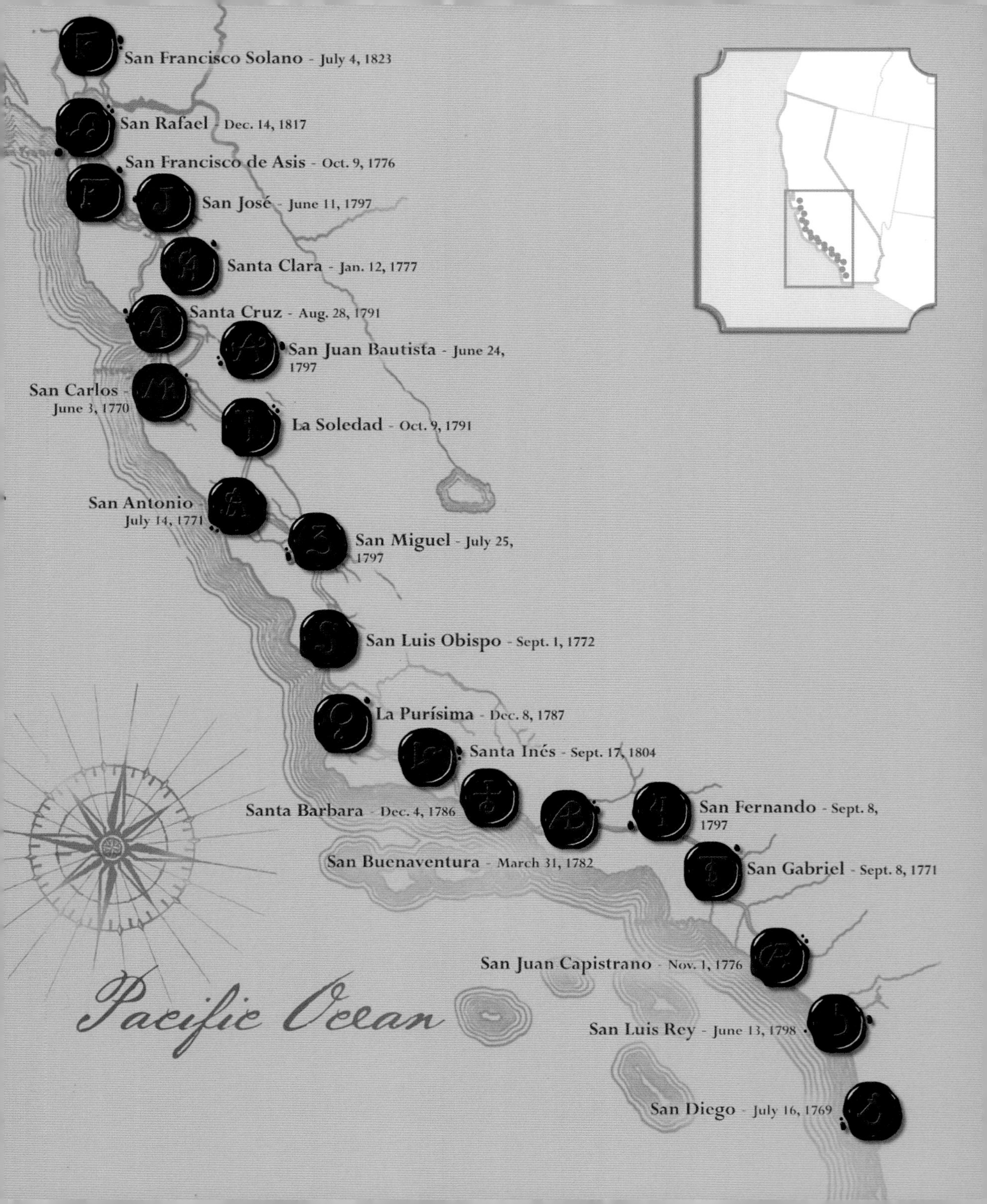

San Francisco Solano - July 4, 1823
San Rafael - Dec. 14, 1817
San Francisco de Asis - Oct. 9, 1776
San José - June 11, 1797
Santa Clara - Jan. 12, 1777
Santa Cruz - Aug. 28, 1791
San Juan Bautista - June 24, 1797
San Carlos - June 3, 1770
La Soledad - Oct. 9, 1791
San Antonio - July 14, 1771
San Miguel - July 25, 1797
San Luis Obispo - Sept. 1, 1772
La Purísima - Dec. 8, 1787
Santa Inés - Sept. 17, 1804
Santa Barbara - Dec. 4, 1786
San Fernando - Sept. 8, 1797
San Buenaventura - March 31, 1782
San Gabriel - Sept. 8, 1771
San Juan Capistrano - Nov. 1, 1776
San Luis Rey - June 13, 1798
San Diego - July 16, 1769
Pacific Ocean

Contents

Foreword

The architectural history of California's twenty-one Spanish missions is one that spans sixty years and 500 miles of California's frontier coastline and plains. It presents a rich and varied source of ancient ecclesiastical and liturgical architecture originating in Spain with local artisans constituting the pre-eminent craftsmen source for the architectural traditions first introduced to the New World. These sources were the heirs of a centuries-long design evolution engendered and enriched by Mediterranean, North African, and Islamic influences born through trade and conquest. A primary source for the tradition was that of the *Ten Books of Architecture* by Vitruvius, a Roman architect in the first century.

Along with the influence of Spain's European and classic traditions were those of New World origin and native peoples inspiration in the design and construction of the California missions. New World considerations were expanded to accommodate a host of construction challenges, including seismic and fire-resistant construction methods, limited resources and materials, and the codification of ceremonial standards and plans for church architecture and iconography.

To help them with addressing local conditions, many friars recruited master stonemasons, carpenters, craftsmen, soldiers, and the occasional Royal Engineer into their employ on the frontier. By the time of the evangelization of Alta California in the late eighteenth century, the architects of New Spain operated on a defined set of design principles and building practices that dictated building proportions, mass and volume, sacred geometry, axial orientation, ornamentation and surface treatments, wall heights, foundation depths, and the use of levers and scaffolding in construction. The religious art and architecture of that era was seldom signed or ascribed to specific architects or patrons, and hence the anonymity of those who played some role in the design will remain a mystery.

Today our emerging understanding of the artistic and architectural contributions and rich histories of the California missions will continue to draw both scholarly and popular interest. We now have a greater appreciation of the California missions and a better understanding of the effects of long-term neglect and unsympathetic historic preservation. This interest has created a need for better documentation. It is important that future generations know these sacred and historically significant places that constitute the measure of the earliest frontier experiences of California and the West.

Cabrillo Landing, painting

This book fills a long-awaited need for documenting the current condition of the grea architectural resources inherent in the upper California missions, along with showing their appealing and mysterious charm, and colorful history. The measured architectura drawings, historic paintings, and early illustrations, along with rare historic photographs assemble a complete visual record of the architecture of the California missions, which until now has not been available in one volume.

Ruben Mendoza PhD.
California Missions Foundation
Carmel, California
2012

Mission San Francisco de Asís

Sources and Precedents for the Missions in the Mediterranean World

Parthenon, Athens, Greece, 400 B.C.

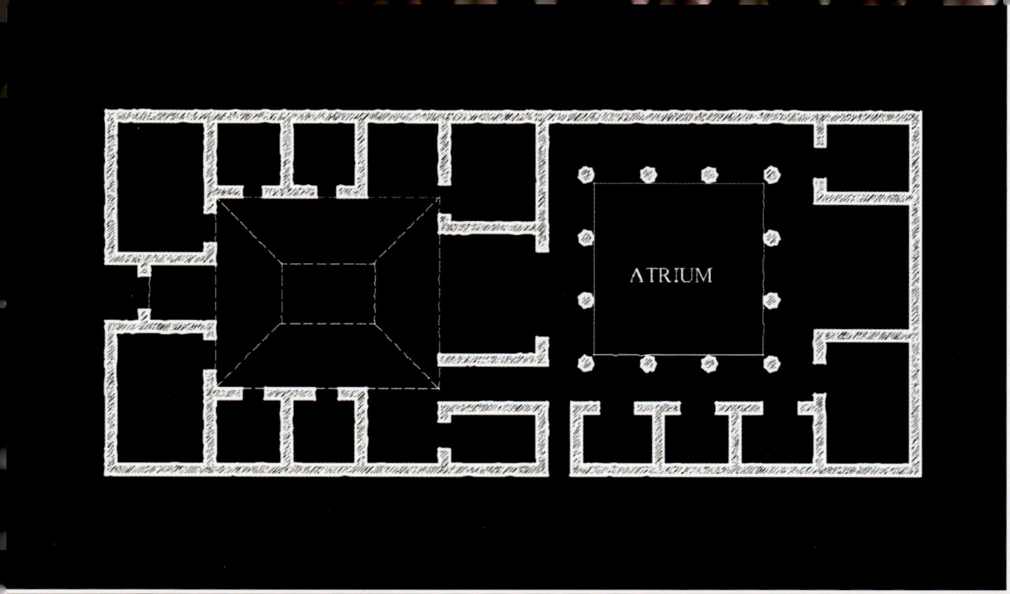

Pompeii, Italy 79 A.D.

Mission La Purísima

The Atrium Plan: Fresh Air and Sunshine

The Greek and Roman systems of planning relied on the use of axes and symmetry to organize their space.

Their invention of the atrium plan, shown here at Pompeii, lent itself to centrally-planned structures with patio courtyards open to the sky, thereby providing light, airy, private, and secure interior spaces. Such linear structures consisted of open, simple post-and-beam covered spaces with masonry walls. The interior courtyard plans of Spain evolved into cloisters and gardens with arcaded peristyles, covered porches, and paved circuits at the perimeter of the early monasteries. Mission friars introduced such atriums and courtyard plans into the New World context for the purposes of protection and security, as well as to provide a sense of community and place in remote frontier settlements. Since the climate of California was akin to that of the Mediterranean world, relatively mild, the Mediterranean open plan traditions could be continued in California.

Aqueduct, Segovia Spain, second century

Adobe mud blocks drying

The Role of the Arch

The discovery of the arch, shown here in Roman ruins, was a breakthrough in design because it allowed large spaces to be spanned with small self-supporting modular elements using simple, usually local, materials. The discovery of the dome vault, an extension of the arch, soon followed, which was ideal for the missions since it provided the means to span great broad volumes in adobe bricks without massive beams or stone lintels.

The long, stacked arcade of the Segovian aqueduct in Spain was a Roman product, but foretells the way the mission's foreign expansion would proceed centuries later. Mission San Juan Bautista's architecture mirrors the same proportions and cadence as the ancient arched screen.

The walls consisted of thick adobe, surrounded at the perimeter with covered arcades paved with terracotta tile. Vaulted adobe domes and arches often served as the crossing for church transepts. Roofed with redwood beams and barrel shaped tiles, the missions could be made entirely with locally available materials.

San Juan Bautista entry arcade

The Arch as a Byzantine Design Element

The expressive architectural use of the classic combination of column, dome, and arch was initiated by the ancients of the Middle East at Petra and Ephesus. Even though this motif has been found in early Rome, the Byzantines used it even earlier, often in Morocco, long before the Renaissance wave of building in fifteenth-century Europe.

On this page is depicted the eighth-century Kairouan mosque in Tunisia, which predates, yet favorably compares with, the best works of the Renaissance (right). Such masonry demonstrates the expertise and creative ingenuity of the craftsmen of that arid, treeless region where long beams and stone columns were scarce, but mud bricks were dirt cheap. Also depicted on this page are views of early but fine Byzantine brickwork and masonry archways of the thirteenth century church on the island of Torcello in Venice.

A Moroccan mosque of the eighth century, Kairouan, with columns supporting a horseshoe-arch between pilasters.

A fine masonry arch of the fourteenth-century Byzantine church built on the Venetian isle of Torcello.

The Borghese Palace was built in 1680 in Baroque Rome. It shows the continued use of the arch with detached columns in the classic pattern.

Mission San Juan Capistrano, scale model of original courtyard.

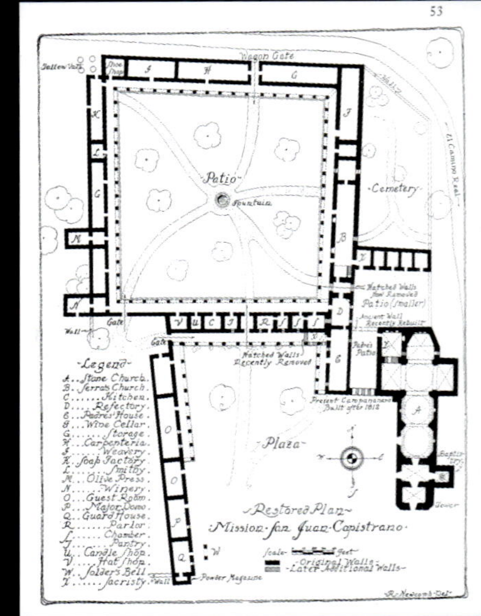

Plaza courtyard of San Juan Capistrano, California

Ninth-century Mosque of Kairouan, Tunisia, with plaza cortile courtyard.

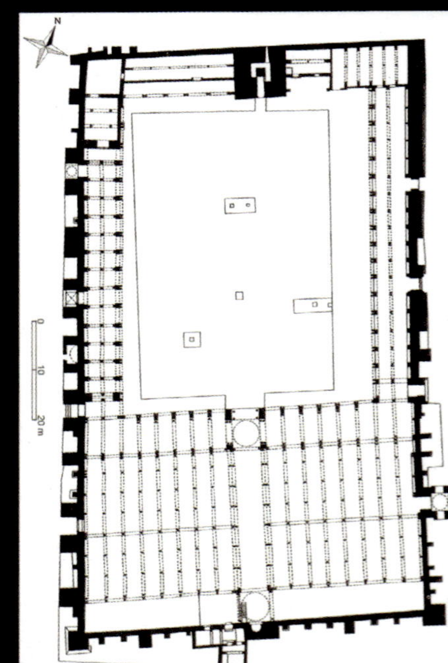

Site plans for the mosque of Kairouan, ninth-century, Tunisia. Note the similarity in layout between the mission and mosque

The arch, when used in a continuous series, becomes an arcade. They were used regularly in history as perimeter porches for the courtyard gardens of any size, from an intimate private atrium walled garden to the wide-open colonnaded courts of the mosques and missions. Interior courts not only served to separate and protect people and property but also to provide a central enclosed space. The sense of community and security engendered in these enclaves was a great contribution to the stability of mission life, and helped in a real way to establish the solidarity of their purpose.

This eighth-century minaret is a close cousin of the stepped-tower at San Carlos Borromeo, in Carmel California (right). This mosque is in the Holy City of Kairouan in Tunisia. The Arabic influence reached central Spain, from which the friars emigrated to the New World. The design vocabulary from which they drew would have had a great deal of Moroccan and Byzantine architectural elements.

Mission San Carlos Borromeo, stepped North Tower, circa 1797

Yucatan parish church, seventeenth century

San Gabriel Mission

The Influence of Native American Design on Spanish Mission Architecture

The influence of the Native Americans on Spanish Colonial church design is profound and invigorating. Their work is found throughout the Yucatan Peninsula and other ancient areas, and can be seen in the parish colonial designs built with great flair and playfulness in their façades.

The best example of Native influence on Spanish mission architectural features is the classic pierced-wall bell tower, *campanario*, such as the one used in San Gabriel Arcángel and then continued to be used as a feature in other missions up the coast. The same element is found in earlier rural churches all over the Southwest, New Mexico, and in Yucatan, predating its use in the California missions by at least half a century. These fluid shapes and bulbous forms are found only in a few Moorish Mudejar churches of Northern Spain, and then again in the outpost rural Native American Spanish parish churches. The Spanish brought the idea of bells, but the bell towers were designed with a more indigenous, primitive form, adding great interest and delight to the more formal, restrained classical forms used by the Friars.

Laguna Mission, New Mexico, c.1700

This striking bell wall at Mani in Yucatan (which was probably built on top of an existing earlier wall) is dated by inscription to 1752. These pierced *campanarios* were once thought to be only found in Alta California, where the first mission was built in 1769. It turns out such pierced-wall *campanerias* occur in Northern Spain, early California, and in earlier seventeenth-century Southwest contexts such as the area of New Mexico and in the Yucatan Peninsula.

The sanctuaries of the beautifully preserved designs of seventeeth-century Pueblo Mission churches San Francisco de Asís at Taos (right), and its counterpart at San José de la Laguna (above) in New Mexico. The Pueblo mission churches of the Southwest and those of the Maya in the Yucatan were built well before those of early California.

Pueblo Indian and Yucatan Area Spanish Churches Predating California Mission Architecture

Cathedral, Salamanca, Spain, seventeenth century

South Tower, Carmel Mission, 1812

Tower Domes

Use of the Moroccan dome demonstrates the Arabic imprint on Spain, which in turn was introduced to the New World.

The domed south tower of Mission San Carlos Borromeo closely resembles that of Salamanca, albeit on a reduced scale. Father Junípero Serra is known to have visited Salamanca, and would have been familiar with this architectural tradition. Fr. Serra was headquartered, and ultimately buried, at San Carlos Borromeo in Carmel.

Mosque Dome, Tunisia. This domed structure is that of the eighth-century Great Mosque of Keh. This architectural tradition served as a prototype for the tower of Salamanca, Spain, in the Middle Ages.

Arcaded Porch with a Window Wall Above

Hospital of the Foundlings, Florence, Italy, by Filippo Brunelleschi, 1450

Santa Barbara Mission, padres quarters, c.1800

Mission San Juan Bautista, 1812
(opposite)

Renaissance Design Influenced the Missions Design which Carried Forward to Today

Classical Roman and Renaissance designs blended with Moorish influence in the inspiration of early California mission architecture. In turn, the missions themselves became a source of inspiration for future Californian architecture. The influence of the mission's style on future California architecture cannot be underestimated or overstated. The mission-typical motif which incorporates low gabled roofs and flat plane building features were inspired by fourteenth-century Florentine design patterns invented by great architects like Filippo Brunelleschi at San Lorenzo in Florence. Another Florentine church, that of Santa Maria Maddalena by Sangallo in the same era, is quite similar to that of San Juan Bautista, dated 1812. These inspirations for the massing of architectural features were then used two centuries later in buildings like the Athenaeum at Caltech in Pasadena, California, by Gordon Kaufmann (1928). The universal appeal of these forms draws on the romantic, historic, picturesque, and economical characteristics of these styles, and speaks to their suitability to the Mediterranean-like climates of California.

Kaufmann was one of many fine American architects charmed by the style. From 1910 onward, mission-styled Mediterranean architecture has been used and immortalized by the likes of good architects like Goodhue, Neff, Mizner, and Smith, to great effect. It set the scene in California development. Mission-styled architecture went on to inspire a host of building types, including country clubs, train stations, city halls, and many private estates.

Santa Maria Maddalena de Pazzi, Florence, Italy, by Giuliano da Sangallo, 1492

The Caltech Athenaeum, 1928, by Gordon Kaufmann, showcases the finest Renaissance and Mission principles of design in this fine setting.

Pedimented Elevations

A fine example of historic classical influence on mission architecture is represented in the façade of the Santa Barbara Mission. Its triangular Roman pediment set atop Corinthian columns is a favorite Vitruvian design element, its pedigree is easily identifiable.

The Greek Parthenon in Athens and Rome's Pantheon of 170 A.D. were among the first buildings to use a pediment placed atop columns. This picturesque and durable combination was used all over the world, especially during the Renaissance by Palladio and his followers. His famous church, San Giorgio Maggiore in Venice, set on the Venice lagoon facing the Piazza San Marco, captivated centuries of admiring tourists and clergy. They took the idea back to their homelands to use in their own buildings. This combination of columns and pediment was used again in Palladio's Villa Barbaro at Maser in the Veneto about 1580. These buildings of his were well known and have been copied widely ever since the 1580s. These buildings became popular prototypes predating the missions by 200 years.

The Friars were not only intrepid pioneers, they were also literate, educated, and often well-traveled. The governing clergy would have been familiar with many of the published and popular great church landmarks of Western Architecture. They brought with them good design ideas tried and true, then simplified its European expression to suit local frontier circumstances. They imported their good taste, their iconic building ideas like the Pantheon, and cultural refinement, which were brought to bear on local construction. They were limited only by the simple tools, unskilled craftsmen, and local materials used in the open country. In addition, they had a genius for selecting the most beautiful sites available from a wide open pristine countryside.

Pantheon, Rome, 100 A.D.

Santa Barbara Mission

Spanish Renaissance Eighteenth-Century Influence on Mission Design

Mission San Luis Rey

Moorish influence is clear from their use of domes, plain extended walls, and bare façades. However, the planning and massing of volumes, shown in the deployment of twin towers or honoring the central axis of the nave, was determined to a great degree by Christian ecclesiastical rituals and iconographic traditions.

On the top left is the church at Cadiz, Spain, one of the oldest historic city ports in the world. Established in Roman times, Cadiz was used as a home port by Columbus when he left for the New World. Its mosque, domed towers, and strong massing would have been a familiar sight to centuries of travelers and missionaries.

Completed in 1815, the Mission Church of San Luis Rey de Francia exhibits the same Moroccan flair, playful wall profiles, and half-moon arcs and domes seen in those of Cadiz's exterior, and also can be identified in the similarity of Sanctuary crossings and baptisteries.

Mission Influence on American Architecture

Inspired by the traditions of Spain and the Mediterranean, mission-style architecture swept California and Florida in the wake of the Panama-American Exposition of 1915, which celebrated the opening of the Panama Canal. It peaked in the 1920s after the Arts and Crafts Movement declined, and prior to the Great Depression, when new construction came to a virtual standstill. Before the Depression, conditions were ideal for growth: there was an economic boom, beautiful building sites were everywhere with big budgets, good craftsmen and architects were in abundance. When construction picked up again after World War II, the mission style was considered passé. At that time Modern International Style took hold in the form of rigid post-and-beam conformity. The Mediterranean-style influence went into eclipse for fifty years.

By the time it returned to popularity in the 1980s, the mission style had degraded to a conventional, generic, and ubiquitous red tile roof style used for everything from shopping centers to motels. Hacienda style subdivisions came along to carpet Southern California. During the economic building boom of the early 2000s, large, mission-styled estates became popular but unfortunately often lacked the detail and panache so characteristic of the work of the better architects of the 1920s. Although its original artistic merit and understated simple grace have diminished, the mission style remains popular today. Fortunately, the best earlier architectural examples are now appreciated and actively preserved as landmark structures by architectural foundations designed to protect them.

The southwest or courtyard-oriented wall of the Mission Church of San Juan Bautista exhibits the strength and massive character of the architectural elements used in the early-nineteenth-century design. This architectural composition, consisting of a central doorway flanked by a pair of matching windows, reflects a favorite feature of the traditional mission vocabulary.

San Juan Bautista with thick adobe walls and a central entry flanked by twin windows.

Santa Barbara Mission, 1831

Everglades Club, Palm Beach, Florida, 1925

Milestone Motel, San Luis Obispo, California, 1925

If the sincerest form of flattery is imitation, then the Santa Barbara bell tower is highly regarded indeed. The original Mission Santa Barbara tower may be seen in the image at top left, whereas an almost identical one designed by Addison Mizner for the Everglades Club of Palm Beach, Florida, may be seen at top right. Above, the first highway motel ever built at San Luis Obispo, California, also installed a tower modeled after that of Santa Barbara. Image at bottom is the motel in its prime.

Flintridge, California, 1928

Wallace Neff, San Marino, California, 1928

George Washington Smith, Casa Herrera, Santa Barbara, California

Mission-Style, Residential Architecture at Its Peak

California architecture was in its prime in the 1920s. With the best sites, the most talented architects, old world craftsmen, and big budgets, the mission style peaked between the two world wars. A prominent architectural feature of this style included broad wall areas with characteristically small windows with elaborate iron grillwork. According to mission historian Dr. David Gebhard, the architects of this style were schooled to not "be afraid of a wall." Many architects who designed with the mission style in mind certainly were not shy about using large wall masses, which often left the interior a little dark due to the emphasis on creating a simple picturesque façade.

Maro Largo, by Joseph Urban, Palm Beach, Florida

Florida's Gold Coast may have had a more flamboyant approach to the mission style decoration, but the massing of its estates and character remain the same. The introduction of the mission-style Mediterranean was mainly due to Addison Mizner. Addison Mizner, who traveled about California in the wake of the Gold Rush of the 1840s, learned about and brought the mission style to Florida, and in so doing became its premier architect and developer.

Florida Estates, Ocean Avenue, Palm Beach Florida

Mission San Jose

Hearst Castle, by Julia Morgan, San Simeon

Palm Beach Train Station, Florida

Santa Barbara Courthouse, by William Mooser, 1929

Mission Architecture Had a Widespread Design Influence Which Peaked in the 1920s

A popular design prototype of the California-based mission style was a massive, low pitched gabled roof with a central entryway and square towers. Examples include such fine large-scale buildings as that of the Palm Beach Train Station, Hearst Castle in San Simeon, and the Santa Barbara Courthouse. All of these structures were erected during the 1920s.

Characteristics of Mission-Style Architecture

Franciscan Mission Architecture of California, 1916 (condensed)

by Rexford Newcomb, from *The Old Mission Churches and Historic Houses of California, 1925*

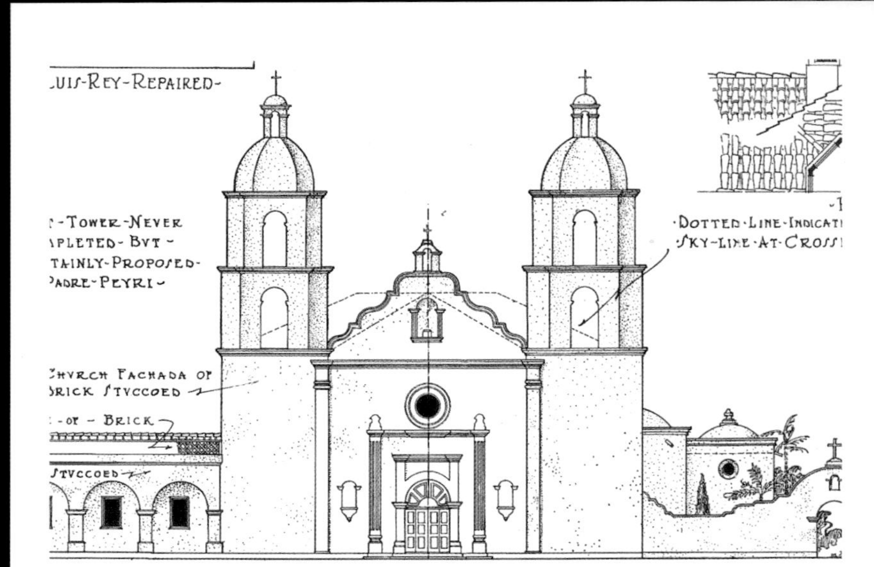

Mission San Luis Rey de Francia, California. — Restoration of the Facade

Of course the purpose of their establishment was to Christianize and civilize the Indian population and to this end each mission establishment was in charge of two priests, one of whom superintended the manual labors, the teaching of the arts, and managed the farm, while the other attended to the spiritual needs and book learning of the Indians. To meet the program requirements placed upon it, the building for a mission must be especially designed. Since there were no architects in the country and few if any artisans (usually craftsmen of any variety had to be brought from Mexico) the padres themselves were obliged to design and superintend the construction of the buildings.

The mission system required first of all of course a church, then priests' quarters, shops for workmen, servants' and soldiers' quarters, convent for the young women, guest rooms, store rooms, refectory, kitchen, etc. The priests must have supervision and access at all times and the establishment must be capable of protection from attacks from without. Hence the arrangement around an open court or patio seemed the solution. This is the plan of all missions that had any pretensions at all. The patio served a very utilitarian purpose and at the same time had an admirable artistic purpose in unifying the plan. In case of attack from without all could be gathered into the patio for protection, and in the apex of the mission period (1800 to 1822) the patio at any mission presented, no doubt, an appearance of ever vari-colored activity.

It will be seen that here was the center of mission private life, while the plaza was the center of community social life. On the plaza were located the priests' quarters, soldiers' quarters, refectory, guest-rooms and offices, while the servants' quarters, refectory, kitchen, larders, storehouses and shops flanked the patio.

1. Patio plan with garden or fountain.
2. Solid and massive walls, piers, and buttresses.
3. Arcaded corridors.
4. Curved and pedimented front gables.
5. Terraced bell-towers, with lantern.
6. Pierced wall, campanario, bell towers.
7. Wide, projecting eaves.
8. Broad, undecorated, wall surfaces.
9. Low, sloping, red-tile roofs.

In conclusion, it can be said that these buildings exhibit unusually fine proportions, obtained in spite of poor materials, lack of skilled workmen and rude implements. In view of the fact that these buildings were designed by laymen, it seems wonderful that such charming results should have been obtained.

Typical Architectural Details Characteristic of the Mission Style

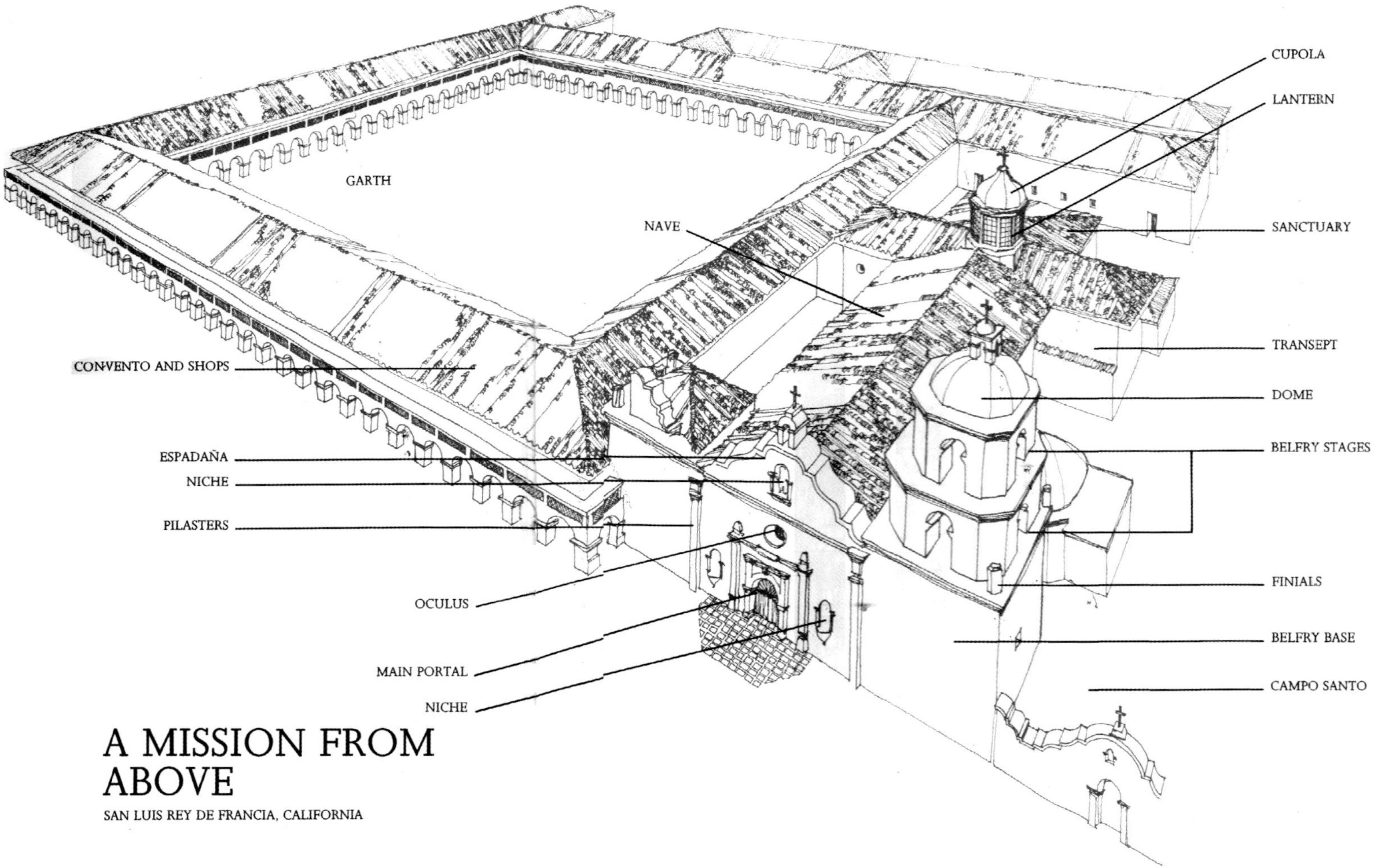

A MISSION FROM ABOVE

SAN LUIS REY DE FRANCIA, CALIFORNIA

Drawing used courtesy of Roger Kennedy

Mission Development Overview

Though the Spanish conquest of Mexico began some 250 years earlier, the main surge of mission development in Alta California took place from 1769 onward. Spanish exploration and colonization is often seen as a Pandora's Box of blessings and curses that changed the continent forever. Spanish conversion and assimilation of the indigenous people who occupied California for thousands of years, along with the occupation of their native lands in an effort to stave off other foreign encroachment, were the hallmarks of the period.

On the good side the Spanish introduced masonry arches, vaulted domes, livestock, and wheat to the New World, however, those benefits were accompanied by a host of problems such as disease, new weapons, and an overbearing clergy to which the indigenous people were vulnerable. While not the result of malice or intent, Native populations soon declined in number and were laid waste by European disease. They were also put to work as forced labor in California and Florida. Native Americans were recruited by all sides, England, France, and Spain, and used as pawns to spur trading, or be guides and soldiers whenever possible.

Once discovered by Europeans, a treasure trove land like North America could not have survived for long as it was. The Spaniards came from the South and the Western sea. As if in a parallel universe, the New England settlers were coming West and compromising the Native peoples from their pilgrim settlements on the East Coast. Everyone recognized the potential value of the new country. Competition for the land and its resources grew heated and fierce.

Except for human nature, one cannot explain why the Europeans felt they had the right to take all the riches and resources after finding the route to this ancient world. In their occupation, they quickly plowed under thousands of years of established civilization for many tribes. On both coasts the Native Americans quickly lost everything in the sweeping tides of change brought on by conquering Spanish, French, and British soldiers. Zealous missionaries and European disease disrupted and closed out their traditional way of life. These were then followed in quick succession by the invasion of gold rush pioneers.

A motivated Spanish clergy arrived in Alta California and immediately undertook the building of many churches, and a few military Presidios, in the period after 1769. These simple, elegant church designs were crafted and raised in colonial outposts throughout the New World of what is now Mexico, the Southwest, and coastal California. Most of the Alta California missions prospered due to abundant natural resources, good management, and plentiful labor. They, in effect, became large ranchos, which were in due course lost in decay and abandoned in the wake of Mexican independence after the 1820s. Secularization came in the 1830s: American colonization was established in the 1840s. Mission properties were then parceled out and sold to private interests over the course of the late nineteenth century.

The lands have fortunately been reassembled as heritage sites in our time, and many have been reactivated as active churches by the Catholic Church. These secular ruins are recognized today as unique architectural treasures by current historians, and the missions are now venerated as the best visible roots of California history as it has come down to us. Moreover, the Church has joined in the effort to recover, restore, and maintain these historic structures and sites. They have cooperated not only in preserving the buildings with integrity but have also, to their credit, continued to nurture the spirit and spiritual base from which they sprang.

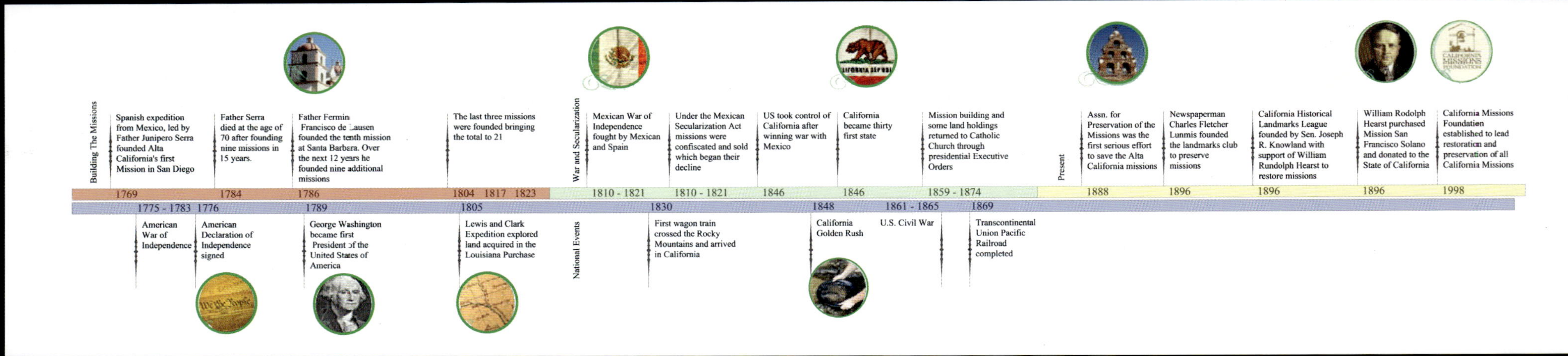

Mission Timeline
Courtesy of the California Missions Foundation

Prehistory

25,000–10,000 B.C.: Peoples of northeast Asia followed herds of caribou, bison, and mammoth across the present day Bering Strait into the American continents.

12,500 B.C.: Santa Barbara Channel Islands were settled; fire sites date from this period.
8,000 B.C.: Settlement of the South California Coast by Chumash. Carbon dated to 7,300 B.C.

Spanish Exploration

1535: Hernando Cortes leads an expedition to Baja and plants a small colony there. It fails after two years and the settlers return to the mainland.

1542: Under the Spanish flag, the Portuguese-born sailor, Juan Rodriguez Cabrillo, became the first European to explore California, landing at San Diego on September 28.

1545: A typhus epidemic kills hundreds of thousands of natives and some colonists in Cuba and New Spain—one of the first of a continued series of European-borne diseases that decimated the native populations.

1669: Gaspar de Portola, governor of the Californians, established a presidio at Monterey, which became the capital of Alta California.

Mission Development

1769: San Diego de Alcalá, the first of 21 missions established by Franciscan padres under the leadership of Father Junípero Serra, was founded. The missions later extend along a 450-mile trail, the El Camino Reál, from San Diego to Sonoma.
1784: Father Serra died after founding nine missions in 15 years.
1785: Father Lasuén founds Santa Barbara and nine more missions.
1812: Russian fur traders established Fort Ross, north of San Francisco.
1820: Ships from Boston began to visit the Spanish towns and Missions came to barter for both otter and beaver pelts.

Mexican Independence from Spain

1821: Mexico wins its independence from Spain, becoming California's new ruler.
1833: Mission lands were confiscated and the land sold into private hands, went into decay.
1839: Wagon trains started to arrive in California, coming overland from the East.

California Statehood

1846: The United States invades Mexico, confiscates area from Texas to California.
1848: James Marshall discovered gold at Sutter's sawmill in Coloma in January. California overrun by Eastern miners coming by boat and overland.

1858: Missions returned to Catholic Church by Presidential Order.
1861–65: U.S. Civil War
1869: September 6, the first westbound train arrives in San Francisco.
1890–today: Mission building's historic value recognized, documented, and preserved as living history, and as active churches.

A Franciscan missionary and founder of the missions of California, Junípero Serra (1713–1784) is one of the most respected and best-known figures in California history.

Junípero Serra was born Miguel José Serra at Petra on the island of Majorca, just off the eastern coast of Spain. Educated by the Franciscan fathers at Palma, Serra joined the order in 1730 and took the name Junípero in memory of a companion of St. Francis of Assisi. For several years following his ordination, Serra remained at Palma as both student and teacher. He received a doctorate in theology in 1742 and served as professor of theology at the Franciscan university in Palma from 1744 to 1749.

Then, at the age of 36, Serra joined a group of missionaries setting out for Mexico. In company with his pupil and friend, Fray Francisco Palóu, Serra arrived in Mexico City in December 1749. Shortly thereafter he volunteered to go to the mission field of Sierra Gorda in northeastern Mexico, where for eight years he served as preacher and teacher. He learned the Otomí language of the natives, built several churches which are still in use today, and established a successful and thriving mission system.

In 1758, Serra prepared for a new assignment at Mission San Sabá on the Texas frontier, but before he could go north, hostile Comanches attacked and burned the mission. The Church then ordered Serra to the Franciscan college of San Fernando in Mexico City, and from 1758 to 1767, he served as home missionary, preached throughout Mexico, and served as a commissioner of the Holy Office, or Inquisition.

Role in California Missions

In 1767, when the Spaniards expelled the Jesuit order from New Spain, Serra became president of the former Jesuit missions in Baja California. He arrived at Loreto in April 1768, and immediately set about the task of improving and enlarging the mission establishments. In 1769, he volunteered to go to Alta California to establish the first missions there. In spite of physical infirmities, he arrived at San Diego in late June 1769, and began construction of the first mission.

During the next fifteen years, Serra devoted his time and energy to the Franciscan establishment in California. His motto was *Siempre adelante*, "always forward." By 1782, Serra had founded nine missions: San Diego, San Carlos Borromeo de Monterey (Carmel), San Antonio, San Gabriel, San Luis Obispo, San Francisco, San Juan Capistrano, Santa Clara, and San Buenaventura. The Native Americans were slowly converted to the Christian religion. In addition to putting them to work building the missions, he taught them trades, introduced domestic animals, and showed them new agricultural methods. The Spaniards believed their European way of life was superior and felt it was part of their mission to educate the native people. The natives in turn had to accept this and adjust to a different way of life or retreat to the hills. Under Serra's direction, the California missions became the most successful and prosperous in all of New Spain.

Not only did Serra have responsibility for the missions, but after the founding of the pueblos of San José and Los Angeles, he also administered the churches there as well as those at the presidios of San Diego, Monterey, San Francisco and Santa Barbara.

Serra died in August 1784 at Mission San Carlos Borromeo and was buried near the altar in the mission church (at present-day Carmel), which has a cenotaph shrine to his memory. Monuments to Serra dot the map from Majorca to San Francisco, and several societies have been established in his honor.

Fermin Francisco de Lasuén

Successor to Fr. Serra

Father Lasuén became a Franciscan (1751) and as a deacon volunteered for the missions of the New World. Upon arriving in Mexico (1759), he entered the Apostolic college of San Fernando. After serving the missions of the Sierra Gorda (1769), he departed for Baja California and remained until 1773, building the mission of San Borja. Traveling overland to the missions of Upper California, Lasuén reached San Diego (1773) and was assigned to Mission San Gabriel until 1775, when he became the personal chaplain to Commander Rivera at Monterey.

Father Lasuén stayed in San Diego until June 1775, when he moved to Monterey. In 1775, Lasuén and Father Gregorio Amurrio were appointed the first missionaries at Mission San Juan Capistrano. When news arrived that the mission in San Diego had been attacked and Father Luis Jayme had been murdered, the soldiers and missionaries hurried back to San Diego. He built a new church there and enlarged the mission compound.

In the summer and fall of 1776, the missions were re-opened and Father Lasuén went with Father Serra to San Luis Obispo, where he stayed until 1777, when he was appointed minister of Mission San Diego. He served there until he became Father-President of the missions in 1785, after Father Serra died. He then moved to the Carmel Mission and stayed there until he died. He was Father-President for eighteen years, and he personally founded nine missions in California. He also expanded many older missions and was responsible for many missions as we know them today.

Though adhering to religious principles, Lasuén was diplomatic in his relationships with the civil and military authorities. Lasuén never adjusted well to life in California and he repeatedly asked for retirement or transfer, stating that only obedience kept him here. Even as he grew older, he kept asking for a transfer or retirement. He never left California, though, and he died at the Carmel Mission on June 26, 1803. He was buried in the sanctuary there.

Serra relics, Mora Chapel, Carmel

nelo (1770)

72)

idio of Santa Barbara: April 1782

Mission Santa Bárbara Virgen y Martir (1786)
Mission La Purísima Concepcion de Maria Sa
Mission La Exaltación de la Santa Cruz (1791
Mission Nuestra Señora de la Soledad (1791)
Mission del Gloriosísimo Patriarca San José (
Mission San Juan Bautista (1797)
Mission San Miguel Arcángel (1797)
Mission San Fernando Rey de España (1797)
Mission San Luis Rey de Francia (1798)

Missions of Alta California

(Presented in the chronological order of their establishment)

San Diego de Alcalá

San Diego de Alcalá, 1769

The First Alta California Mission

The Mission San Diego de Alcalá was the first mission founded in California, and the first of twenty-one missions that make up the chain of missions along the El Camino Reál, or Kings Highway. It was founded on June 16, 1769, by Friar Junípero Serra. It was moved from what is now known as Presidio Hill above Old Town to its present site in 1774, was burned in an Indian attack in 1775, rebuilt in 1780, destroyed in an earthquake in 1803, and enlarged in 1813. The present building is a restoration of the 1813 church that was rebuilt in 1931.

The settlement had many problems the first year. The Native Americans came only to accept gifts and to take unguarded possessions—there was also a great deal of strife and some violence between the indigenous population and the soldiers. Conversions were slow. The mission was almost abandoned that first year due to the lack of supplies and illness. In August of 1774, under Father Luis Jayme, with approval by Father-President Serra, the mission was relocated to its present site six miles east to obtain a better supply of water, more fertile soil, and to get away from the Spanish military presence that intimidated the Native Americans. Each of the missions was built to be one day's walk apart.

The new site was close to the San Diego River and the American Indian villages, but two of the mission Indians became discontented with the rules and regulations and they incited eight hundred to storm the grounds in the middle of the night on November 4, 1775. The mission was burned to the ground and the presiding father was killed—he is now buried under the altar of the present church. The padres, under Father Serra who returned to supervise, rebuilt the mission according to army fort specifications. By 1780, most of the reconstruction of the mission and its outbuilding was completed. The church and other buildings were arranged in a quadrangle around a patio. In 1807, work was begun on a dam six miles upriver that would provide the necessary water for the mission to flourish.

This is the fifth church on this site. The church was enlarged over the years to accommodate the growing population of neophytes (baptized American Indians). In 1812, as the fourth church was being built, a devastating earthquake damaged and destroyed several other missions. In 1813, the church was enlarged and the present church, rebuilt in 1931, mirrors it. Buttress wings were added during the 1813 enlargement to stabilize the façade in the event of an earthquake.

The beginning of the end of the Mission System came in 1821, when Mexico gained its independence from Spain. During the Mexican occupation of California, in the Act of Secularization, various companies of artillery and cavalry were at the mission until 1859. The army used the adobe church as a stable for their horses. They made some repairs and added a second floor to the church. Subsequently, the mission was abandoned for several years.

In 1862, twenty-two acres of the mission lands were restored to the Church by order of President Abraham Lincoln.

In 1892, the Sisters of Saint Joseph of Carondolet moved onto the mission compound and conducted an American Indian children's school for seventeen years.

In 1931, only the façade was still standing and the mission was rebuilt to mirror the 1813 church.

This unusually free-spirited façade set the pace at the first mission. The plaster, top line profile, unusual trim, and bell tower are all influenced by earlier parish churches in the region of the Native Americans in Yucatan and the Pueblo area of New Mexico.

Birds-eye view of a model of the original mission layout, including the barnyards, gardens, and outbuildings.

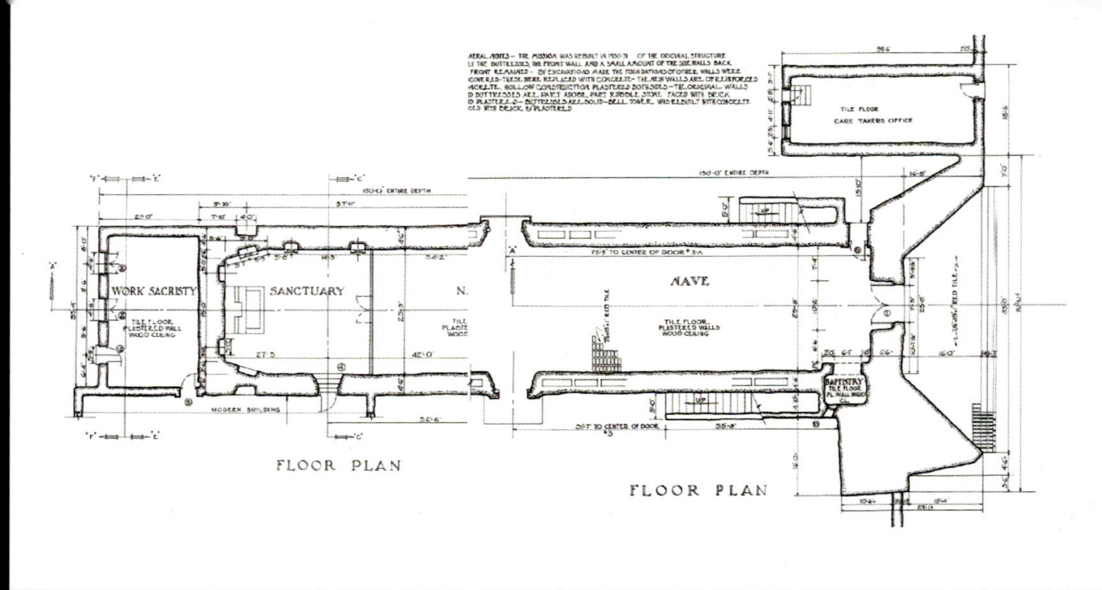

As-built, dimensioned plan of the mission from the Historic American Building Survey (HABS).

View of original mission looking west, most of which has been redeveloped over time.

This Edward Vischer painting of 1870 shows the original country setting of the mission.

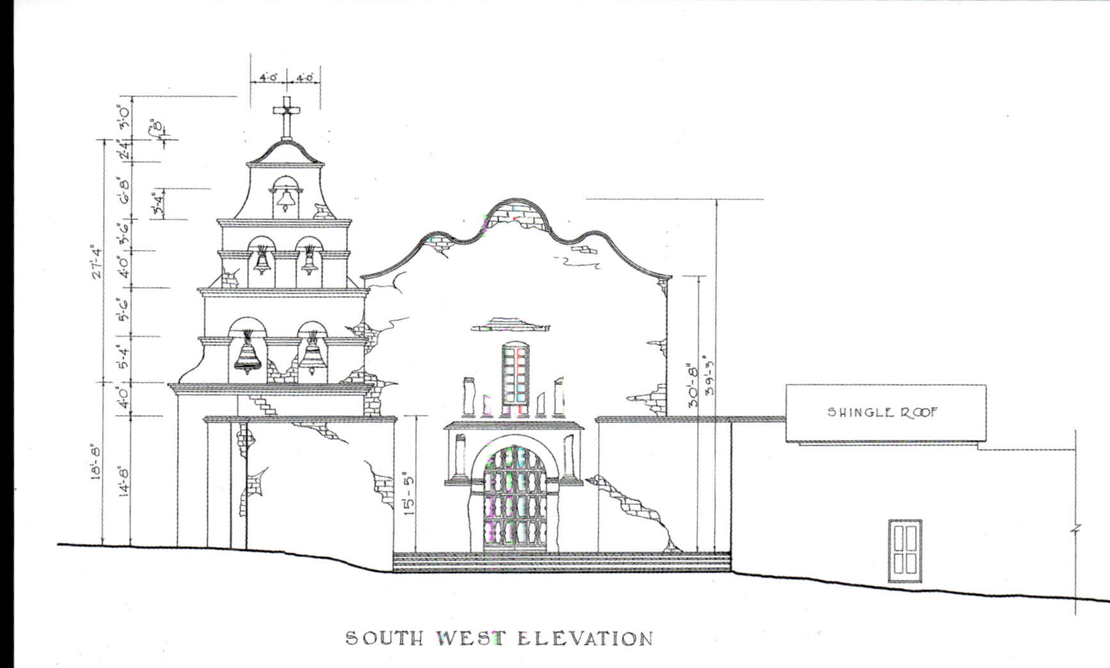

These HABS measured drawings from the 1930s document the mass of the original mission.

Elevation model and site plan of the original mission.

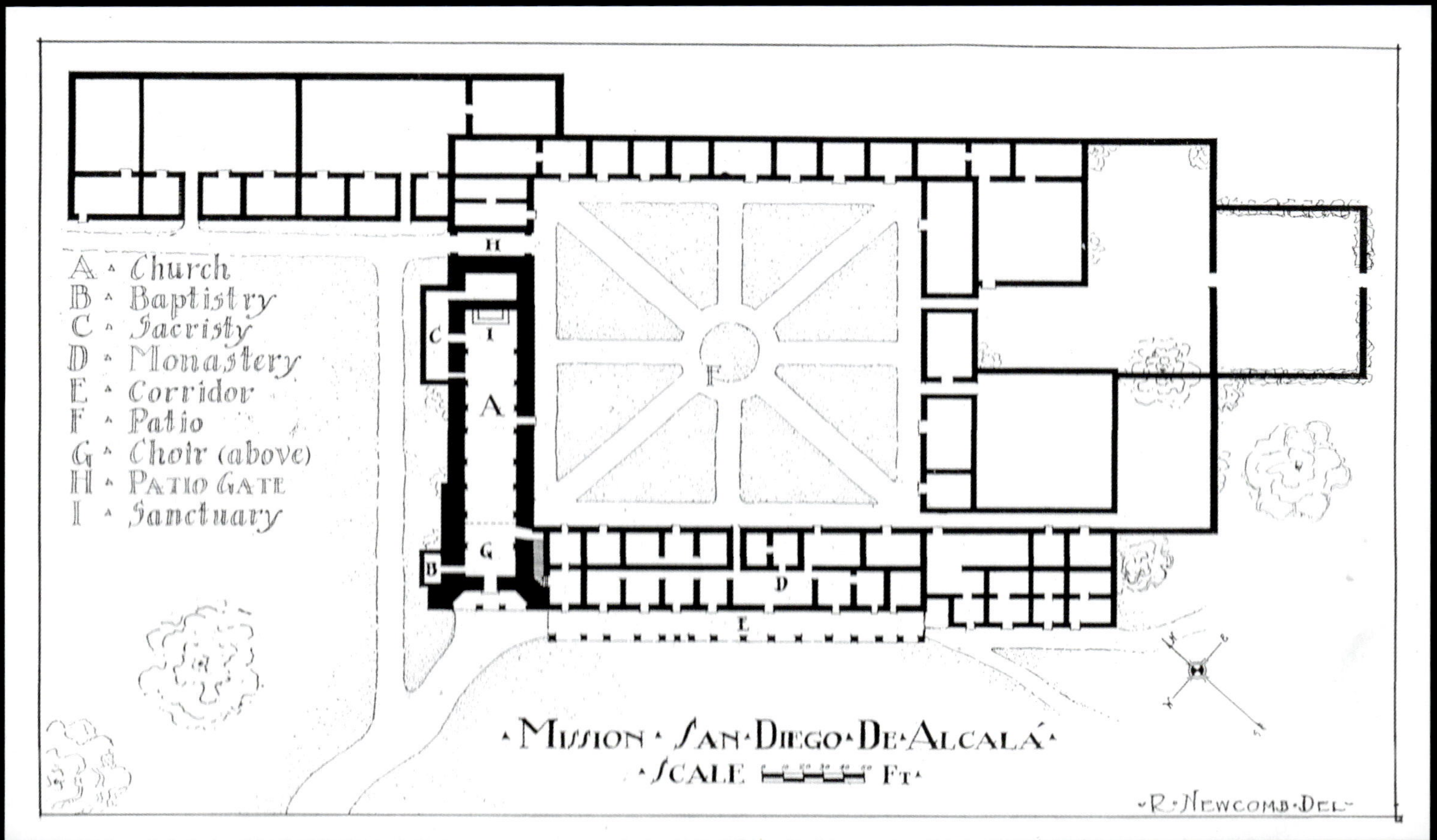

Top Left: The stair entry to the choir is on the exterior.
Center: Main court with arcade.
Bottom left: The side entry to the main sanctuary from the courtyard.

A view of the choir loft and main entry to the mission facing south. The canted walls above create an optical illusion of unevenness inside but echo the slanted wing walls of the exterior.

The large, simple plain wall and tall narrow *reredos* (carved altar), is elegantly proportioned. The wall is further filled out with niches for the sculptural saints and a festive pulpit canopy.

Deep set walls are evident in the overhead beam supports and heavy oak doors with *clavos* (decorative nails).

The terracotta treads and balustrade rail cap give a picturesque look to a utilitarian function.

This famous type of bell tower with a pierced vertical wall for bells is called a *campanario*. It is an architectural feature seen in Mudejar, Spain, and in earlier Yucatan and Native American churches.

These unusual patterns in deep relief reflect the indigenous influence which catch the sun and provide interest to the thick adobe wall of the entry.

San Carlos Borromeo del Rio Carmelo, 1770

San Carlos Borromeo del Rio Carmelo, 1770

This mission is the second to be established in the mission chain, being consecrated in 1771. The current mission structure is the seventh in a series of church buildings that stretch back to the beginning.

The first crude shelter of logs was erected in Carmel after moving from the Presidio of Monterey. Considered the most beautiful of all the California missions, the present rough-hewn stone church reflects the design of a master-mason, brought to a crude perfection by the Native American apprentices.

The first settlement at Monterey was found to be inadequate due to the unsuitability for crops, the lack of indigenous people living around the bay, and the close proximity to the presidio's garrison troops. Friar Serra found the present site on a hillside in Carmel Valley, overlooking a fertile plain close to the sea. Six months later, the first wooden chapel was complete, along with the dwelling, the storehouse, a soldiers' quarters, and a corral; all of this was surrounded by a palisade.

Mission San Carlos Borromeo del Rio Carmelo become Friar Serra's headquarters for the entire mission chain, but he was rarely there, as he spent a good deal of his time traveling to each of the missions spread out over five hundred miles.

Father Serra had planned on a stone church and had ordered the quarrying of stone for it in 1781. It is thought that he even sketched out the design. But he was not to see this completed: on August 28, 1784, Friar Serra died at the age of 71. Friar Serra was interred in the sanctuary near the altar. When the adobe church was replaced by the present stately one of stone, his remains were kept at the same location. Father Lasuén was named his successor and made Carmel his headquarters and base of operations from this location for the next eighteen years.

In November of 1818, two vessels of the pirate Bouchard arrived at Monterey. Four hundred of his men landed and set torch to Monterey and the presidio, but the mission survived. After secularization in 1834, the land around the mission was sold, right up to the walls of the church. Services continued to be held even though the roof beams rotted and gave way in 1851. A shingle roof was built over the church. This steep-pitch roof was criticized but remained in place for more than fifty years, before being replaced with tile. In the 1930s, Harry Downie rebuilt the mission after painstaking research into the physical and written records. The church today is one of the most authentic restorations of the entire mission chain.

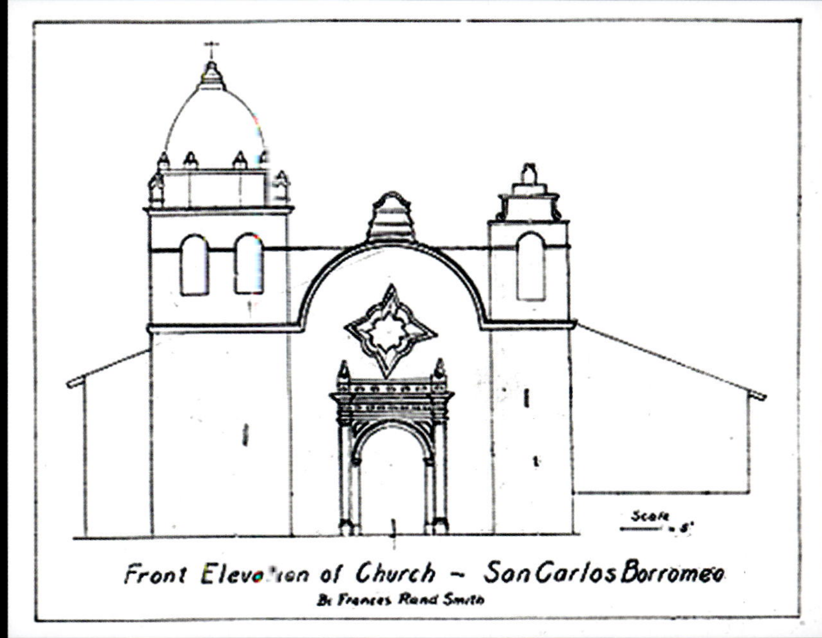

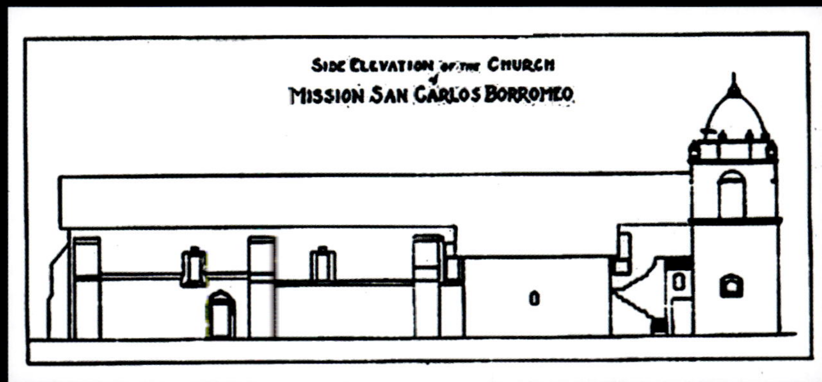

As-built, measured drawings showing the dimensioned elevations alongside the actual building.

Photo by C.W. Johnson c. 1890

A photo (left) and romantic painting (above) show the mission
in its early state. These are historic views of the mission prior to

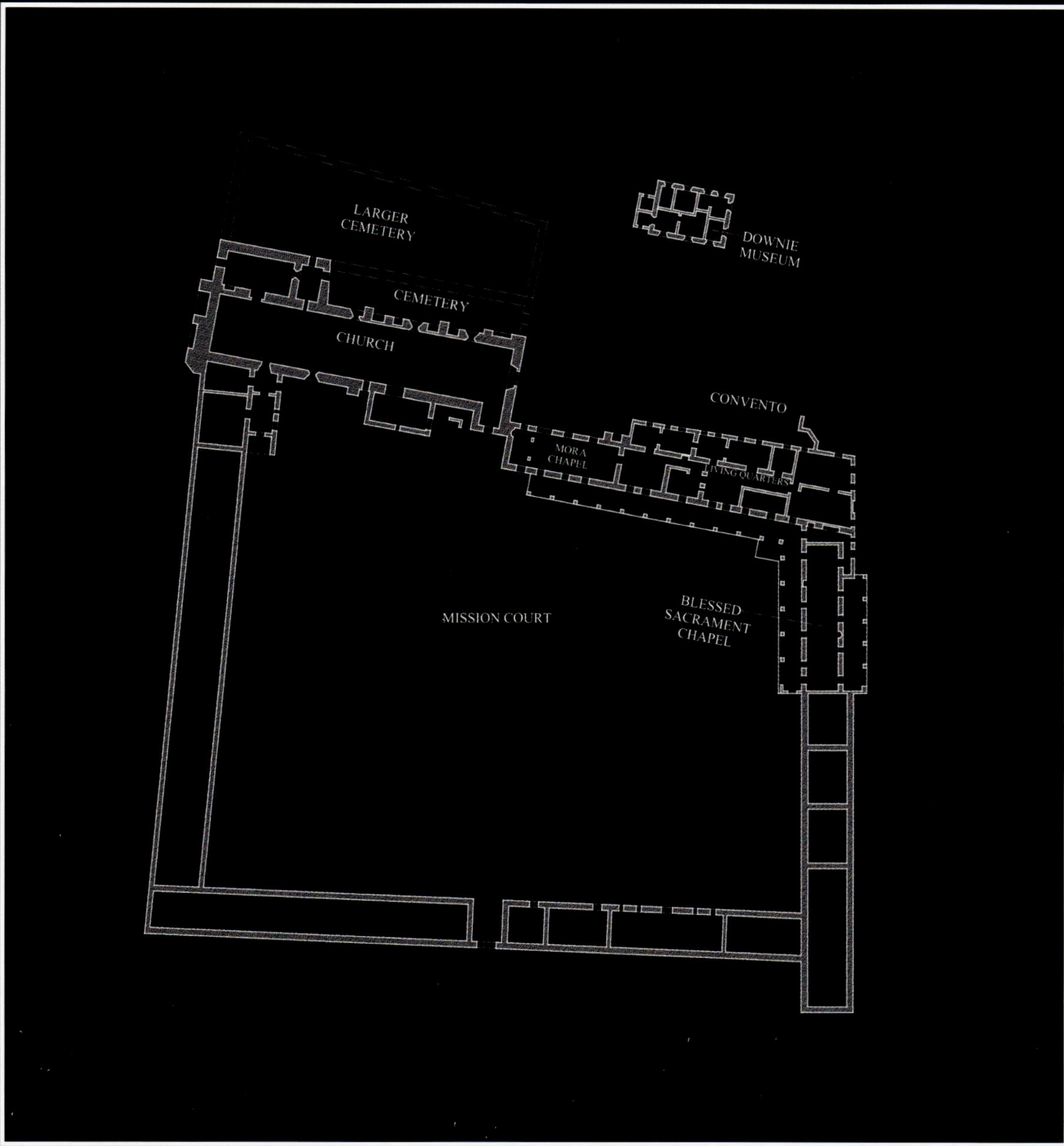

The full quadrangle in its original state.

The south tower elevation toward the courtyard fountain has an egg-shaped dome which can be traced to the Morrocan roots of Spanish architecture.

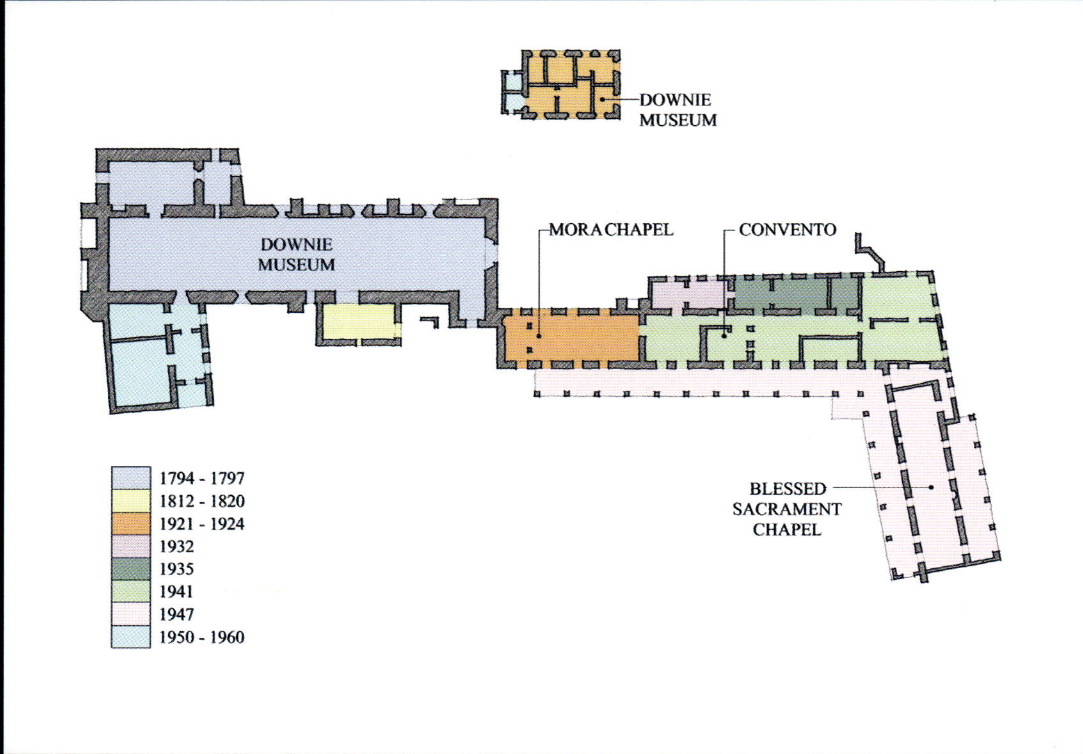

Phases of the mission's development. *Courtesy of the Carmel Mission Foundation.*

The towers, entry and stone trim show the quality of the work. Even in this primitive setting, each element has merit as a separate architectural feature or as a striking composition.

This choir view shows impressive organ pipes above the main entry to the mission sanctuary.

View of the main altar and *retablo* under the unusual, and carefully restored, elliptically shaped vault.

Father Serra is buried in the main church near the altar. This cenotaph is a separate memorial room with praying friars by sculptor Joe Mora. Fr. Serra's relics and artifacts are shown behind glass at the altar.

The carved stonework on this portal entrance into the side chapel survives from the original mission and is considered to be some of the best work found in any of the missions.

The padres' personal apartment shows the well-proportioned cozy elegance they were able to achieve even in this frontier with no conventional societal support.

Ingenious and elegant graphics trim the walls with a delicate and fine sense of color. The pattern is considered by most to be Native

The padres' personal apartment.

The thick wall and small-pane window frame gives the painted recess an artistic flair.

The deep wall opening modulates and reflects the light, trimmed by a simple, deep, and economical plaster frame.

Various shapes and sizes for the windows give the building character and show the talented craftsmanship of the missionary builders.

Incorporating the wall into the patio enclosure unites the composition and creates an integrated, consistent design.

Playful, decorative shapes and simple wood planking make the trim read like furniture, which has interest without being too fussy or ornate.

The plaster walls, projections, and stone stairs give scale and depth to the different architectural elements of the mission.

A variety of the chimney treatments create
visual interest at the roof line.

Fine iron work like this makes a decorative, distinctive feature out of a utilitarian function.

Hand-forged wrought iron, the best for durability, was an art form in itself. It was limited only by the blacksmith's imagination and serves as the building's jewelry.

Mission San Antonio de Padua, 1771

Mission San Antonio de Padua, 1771

Mission San Antonio de Padua, 1771

The Mission San Antonio de Padua is the third mission founded in California. It was founded on July 14, 1771, by Friar Junípero Serra. San Antonio Mission and La Purísima in Buellton are the most characteristic of the original mission settings, as the padres would have lived in them.

Originally, San Buenaventura was to be the third mission, but due to unsettled conditions its founding was delayed, and San Antonio took its place as the third mission. Father Serra chose a spot, a pleasant location with live oaks and alders in the Santa Lucia Mountains, that had caught Governor Portola's eye when he passed through two years earlier.

Father Buenaventura Sitjar was one of the two padres left in charge. He created aqueducts to the mission grounds, which enabled a grist-mill, a mill-race, a fountain, and even a bathing pool. Much of the original water system is still visible to this day, including the original retaining wall of the reservoir. Father Sitjar also created a translation of the Mutsun language, spoken by the natives of the San Antonio Valley, by which they were able to prepare catechisms in the native language.

Upon secularization in 1834, the Native Americans departed after being mistreated. They returned to the mountains and the mission was abandoned for the next 46 years. Being so remote from the routes of travel, the buildings were plundered of all usable construction materials, fell into decay, and became ruins.

In 1903, Joseph R. Knowland of the California Historic Landmarks League started restoration, and after some difficulty they completed restoration in 1907. It has been called "the largest and most picturesque of the remaining missions of Northern California." Restoration hardships were many: heavy rains in 1904–05 washed out the earlier work, an earthquake in 1906 toppled the previous year's work, and in 1907 the lumber could not be delivered due to the muddy roads.

Finally, in 1948, the Hearst Foundation and the Franciscans of California stepped in and took all of the buildings, except the church, to the ground, and painstakingly rebuilt them from scratch. The existing structures were reinforced with steel and concrete, though old materials and methods were used when possible. The current mission is believed to be an accurate replica of the 1813 original, though the fanciful façade was added well after the original construction, which would have been similar to the plain-face gable pattern found throughout the chain.

GARDEN

An historic Watkins photo, c. 1900, shows the mission prior to restoration. The work was funded primarily by the Hearst family, whose San Simeon Castle is on the same part of the coast.

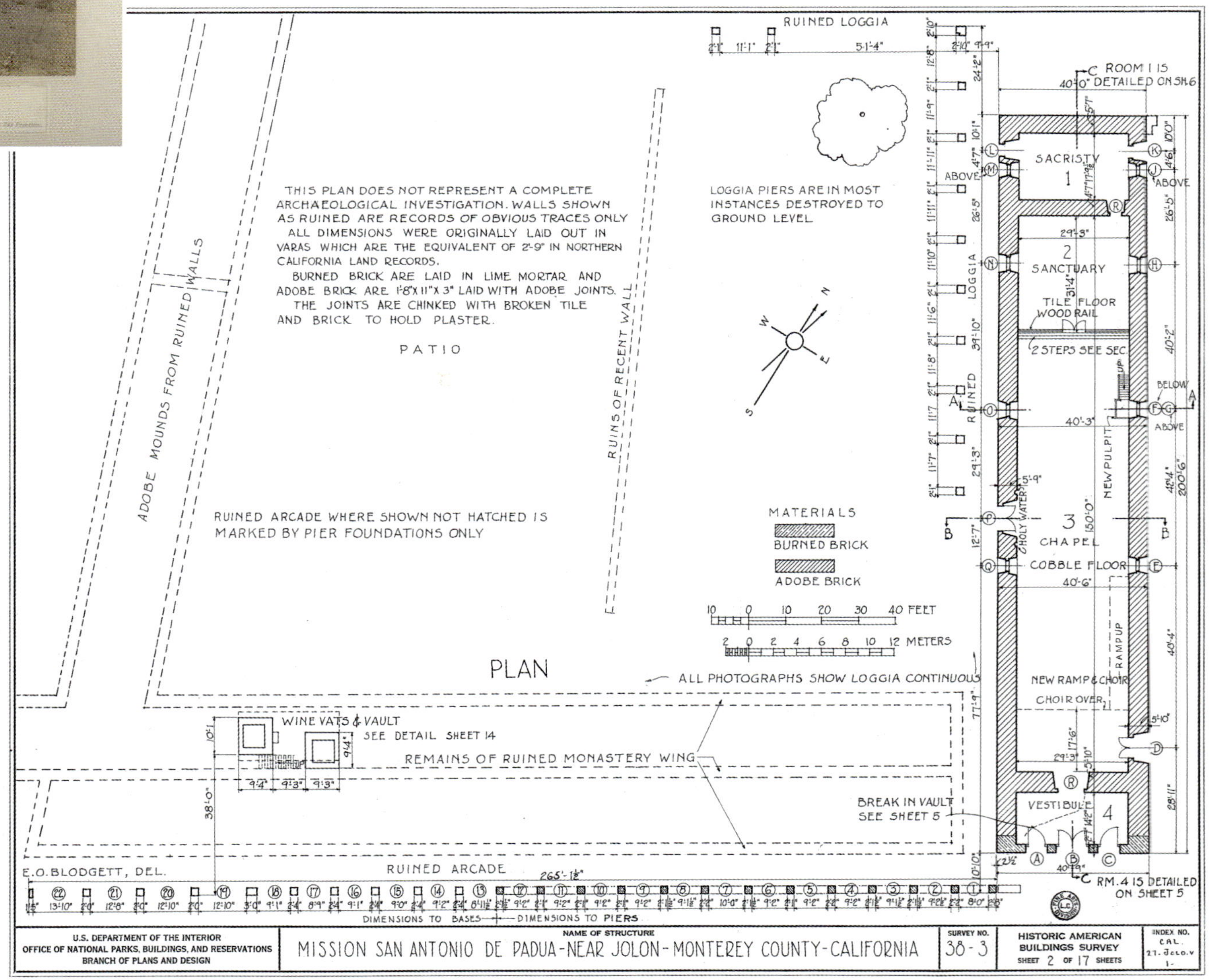

A historical HABS document records the original floor and site plan of the mission.

South and east elevations showing the fancif reconstruction of the principle façade and sweeping proportions of the mission itself.

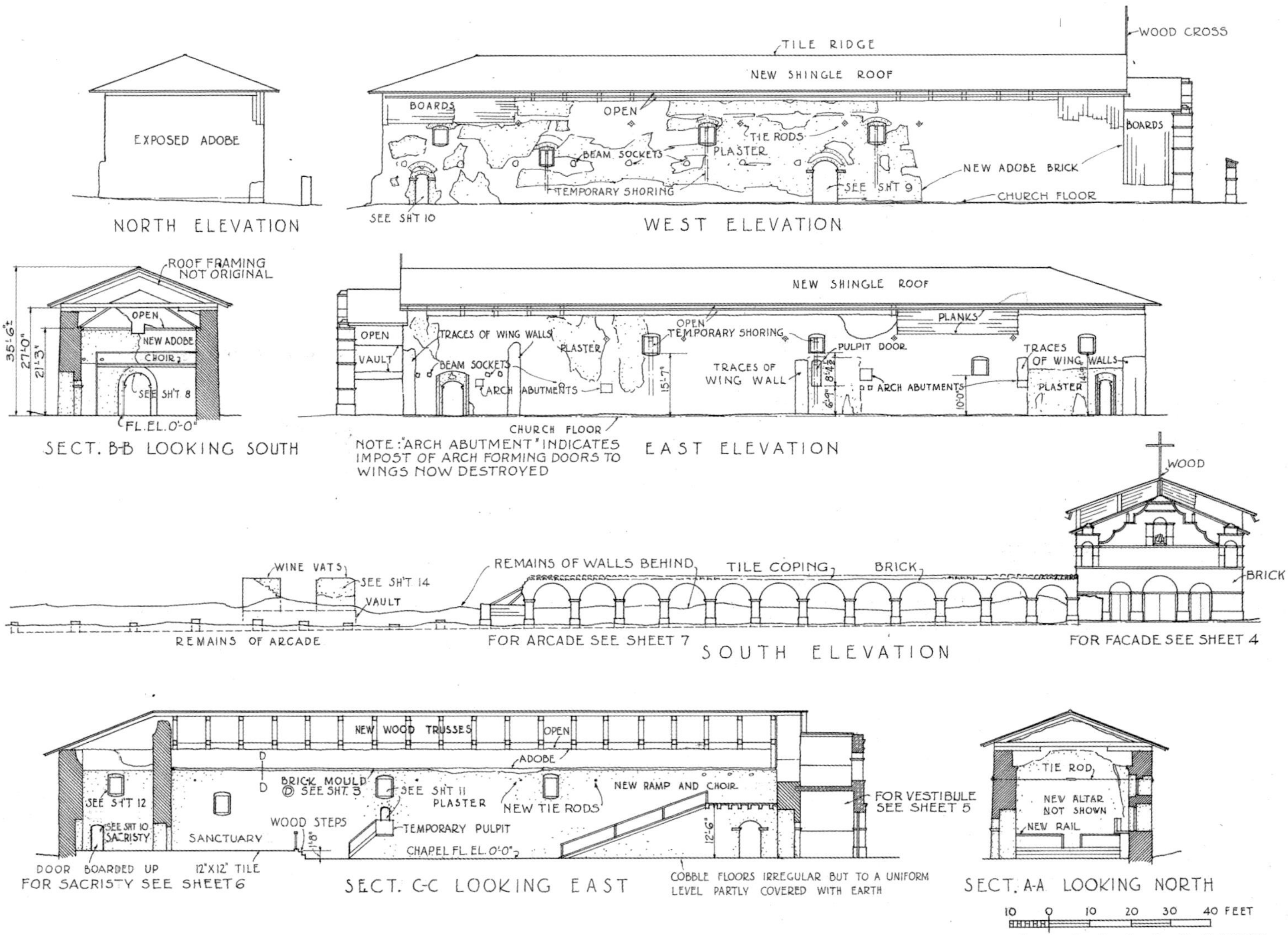

E. O. BLODGETT DEL.

SEE SHEET 17 FOR RESTORED ELEVATIONS

U.S. DEPARTMENT OF THE INTERIOR OFFICE OF NATIONAL PARKS, BUILDINGS, AND RESERVATIONS BRANCH OF PLANS AND DESIGN	NAME OF STRUCTURE MISSION SAN ANTONIO DE PADUA - NEAR JOLON MONTEREY COUNTY CALIFORNIA	SURVEY NO. 38-3	HISTORIC AMERICAN BUILDINGS SURVEY SHEET 3 OF 17 SHEETS	INDEX NO. CAL. 27-JOLO.V 1-

This choir view of the main entry of the corbeled loft shows the simple vaulted gable roof with a bare, plank ceiling; though beautiful, the original ceiling vault may have been different prior to restoration.

Altar view with a simple ceiling and serene painted details. This restoration is believed to come close to the original appearance of the nave.

Restoration of interior rooms showing the original use and axial floor plan of the back rooms.

Making candles in the candle factory.

Baptismal fount in the baptistery

Kitchen

Original adobe *lavanderia* outbuilding on the mission site

Economical and charming, Native American motifs made with leather stencils were used to decorate the mission and make the surroundings seem more familiar and inviting to the new converts.

ed arcades prov

The doubled-up terracotta tile roof and reconstructed *campanario* create a lively pattern on the roof top.

The quatrefoil form of the fountain is characteristic of many mission fountain basins. It was a shape used both in plan and elevation, a favorite of the mission fathers.

Fountains enliven the interior court's atmosphere and provide water to the courtyard. The soft rounded shapes of this fountain are characteristic of the Native American style, giving it a graceful and casual handmade form.

Decorative chimney caps like these made rooftops interesting as they protected the mission from water intrusion.

Architectural details from the old world, like these corbels, give the rooms character and provide a level of comfort and warmth beyond being merely utilitarian.

The sheer elegance of this vaulted wine cellar shows the natural charm and soulful nature of mission architecture. It illustrates the padres' good taste and sophisticated background as they pioneered new construction on the site.

Mission San Gabriel Arcángel

Mission San Gabriel Arcángel, 1771

Mission San Gabriel Arcángel, 1771

The Mission San Gabriel Arcángel is the fourth mission founded in California. It was founded on September 8, 1771. Named for the Archangel Gabriel, the angel of the Annunciation, this mission was one of the most prosperous and often frequented by travelers. The south façade, with its dramatic series of pilasters, replicates the Cathedral of Cordoba.

Sitting astride three well-traveled trails—two from Mexico to Alta California, and one, at a later period, from the East Coast of the United States to California—this mission was a wayside stop for most anyone traveling to California. The mission was constantly overrun by the military, whose behavior constantly tried the patience of the mission fathers. Because of this dynamic, the mission was in constant trouble with the indigenous population.

The mission was founded approximately nine miles east of the heart of present-day Los Angeles, on a site selected by Father-President Serra near the Santa Ana River. It was later moved to the nearby San Miguel Valley, placed upon a hill.

Unfortunately, an incident of misconduct by one of the soldiers destroyed the Native American's confidence in the missionaries and created a lasting hatred of the military. A soldier assaulted the wife of the native chief. To avenge this wrong, the chief attacked and was himself humiliated and killed in the skirmish. It was a long time before the Spanish settlers were trusted again.

In 1772, Father Lasuén visited and recommended moving the mission to a better site. In 1775, the mission finally moved to avoid the spring floods that ruined their first crops. It was a good move, making San Gabriel the heart of an agricultural development area. In effect it was a prosperous rancho. They produced abundant crops of corn and beans, while building great herds of cattle. In addition, San Gabriel became famous for its fine wines.

In 1779, a new church built of stone and concrete was started. Its vaulted concrete roof was eventually cracked by earthquakes and it was replaced in 1805 by a flat tile roof. The church was completed. In 1812, an earthquake damaged the monastery and toppled the church tower, which at the time was at the front of the church. The padres moved into the granary and converted it into a temporary chapel. In 1828, the church was completely restored with its dramatic Renaissance façade. Its unique Moorish design, with a beautiful south wall of impressive and beautifully spaced piers, is inspired by the Cathedral at Cordoba, Spain, where one of the fathers had studied. The new bell tower was erected at the west end of the side wall, which was a beautiful rustic *campanario* composed of three rows of arched openings holding the bells.

Secularization in 1834 destroyed the mission; by 1843, the mission properties were all but ruined, occupied by half-starved Native Americans. In 1859, President Buchanan returned the building to the Catholic Church—it was used as a parish church until 1908, when it became the property of the Claretian Fathers.

This massive block face is the plainest façade possible yet exudes charm and character. The central processional entry is characteristic of all the missions and uses design features of sculpture and plaster decoration to provide accents with symbolic interest.

The beautiful south façade of the mission sanctuary has an unusual line of buttressing pilasters used in a widely admired and architecturally expressive manner. This pattern is similar to the Cathedral "La Mezquita" in Cordoba, built in the tenth century, and is thought to be its source.

An old wooden model of the mission.

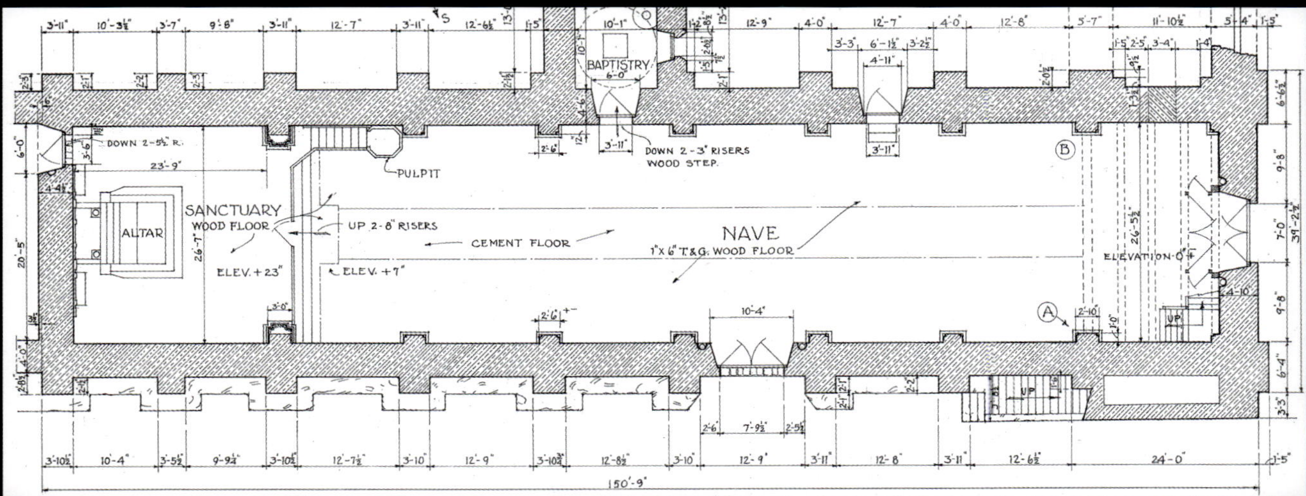

A HABS dimensioned-plan drawing of the sanctuary from 1933.

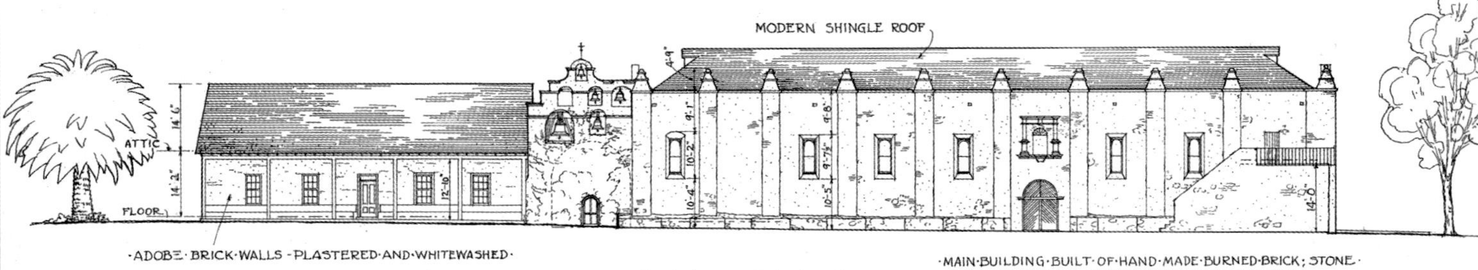

SOUTH ELEVATION

·MAIN·BUILDING·BUILT·OF·HAND·MADE·BURNED·BRICK; STONE·
·AND·LIME·MORTAR; COATED·WITH·THIN·PLASTER·
·SACRISTY·AND·BAPTISTRY·HAVE·MASONRY·VAULTED·ROOFS·
·MASONRY·VAULT·OVER·NAVE·HAS·BEEN·REPLACED·WITH·
·WOOD·ROOF & CEILING·

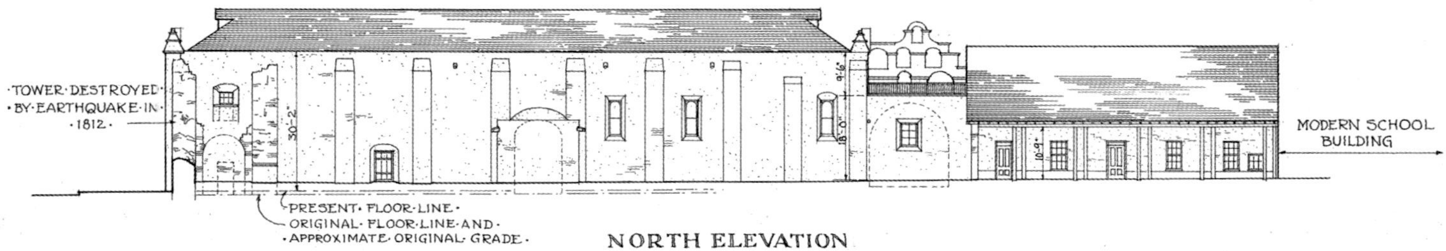

NORTH ELEVATION

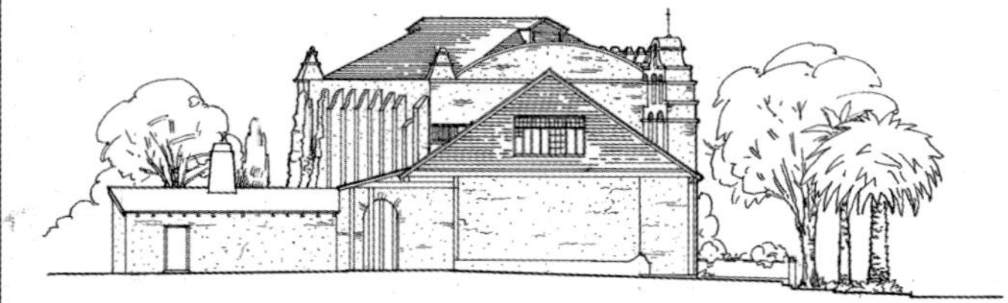

WEST ELEVATION

EAST ELEVATION

FEET 5 0 5 10 20 30 40 50

METRIC 2 0 2 4 6 8 10 12 14 16

FREDERICK SCHOLER, DEL.

U.S. DEPARTMENT OF THE INTERIOR OFFICE OF NATIONAL PARKS, BUILDINGS, AND RESERVATIONS BRANCH OF PLANS AND DESIGN	NAME OF STRUCTURE MISSION SAN GABRIEL ARCANGEL MISSION DRIVE · SAN GABRIEL · CALIFORNIA	SURVEY NO. 37-8	HISTORIC AMERICAN BUILDINGS SURVEY SHEET 5 OF 12 SHEETS	INDEX NO.

The fine craftsmanship using economical and primitive plaster strapping gives the walls character and ethnic charm. Many of these features differ according to the local tribes, thus giving variety and a different look to each mission

The church interior was redone in Victorian times and shows the ornate character of that period.

The dry painted plaster, or *fresco seccos*, in the baptistery shows the painterly approach and fine technique in the dome and dramatic religious symbolism of the Church.

These graceful niches and restrained plaster work show the fine detail and integrated symbolism of the church's decoration.

Mission San Luis Obispo de Tolosa, 1772

Mission San Luis Obispo de Tolosa, 1772

Mission San Luis Obispo de Tolosa, 1772

The Mission San Luis Obispo de Tolosa is the fifth mission founded in California. It was founded on September 1, 1772, by Friar Junípero Serra and named for Saint Louis (b. 1274), a Bishop of Toulouse and the son of Charles II, King of Naples.

In 1769, as Governor Portola's expedition was returning to San Diego from its vain search for Monterey, they came up on a spacious marshy valley with a large population of grizzly bears—they named the place *La Canada de los Osos* ("Valley of the Bears"). In 1772, the missions at Carmel and San Antonio were near starvation and sent hunting parties to successfully kill grizzlies and return with the food.

Father Serra came back to the valley and selected a low hill near a stream of the finest water, where the founding of the mission was completed. There were no native settlements in the valley, but attracted by the building going on, many Native Americans arrived from afar. The local indigenous population were eventually persuaded to be baptized and the colony grew slowly.

Not all of the Native Americans were peaceful, however. In 1776, the padres' quarters were burned along with all the log buildings, except for the church and granary. Flaming arrows shot by enemies of the mission neophytes started the blaze. Forced to deal with these attacks, in 1890, the first tile roofs were manufactured. These roofing tiles were the first made in California and were quickly copied by the other missions.

The principal architect of the mission's prosperity was Father Luis Antonio Martinez, who knew that secularization was coming. Prior to his banishment, he let the property sink into disrepair. With secularization, the Native Americans drove off the livestock and the buildings were allowed to deteriorate, such that by 1845, the mission property could only bring $510. During the Mexican war, Fremont surrounded the building, believing it to be held by Mexican insurrectionists, only to find it occupied by women and children.

In 1859, what was left of the mission was returned to the Church. In 1868, the buildings were remodeled to look like a parish church, with the adobe walls encased in white painted siding and a steeple added. This remained in place until 1934, when it was removed and the building restored to its former simple grace and dignity. The grounds have been greatly reduced by the encroachment of urban development, but the building itself now sits safely restored and serene in a creekside plaza.

This is the south-facing façade, restored in 1933 to its original appearance. The floor plan is L-shaped and a unique form to the missions, which created a convenient, but unfortunately fairly awkward way to expand the church and participate in the church service.

These long colonnades are more reminiscent of Roman columns and lintels than the usual running arcades found in the other missions.

HABS measured elevation drawings of the mission.

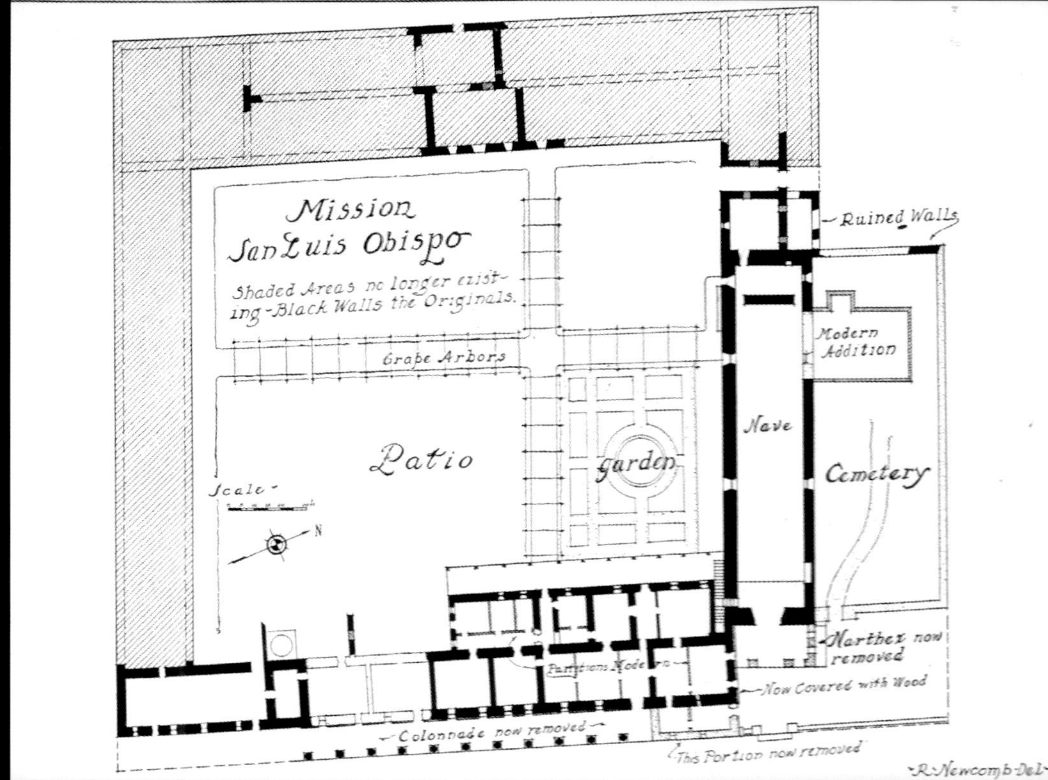

The plan was in the traditional quadrangle form, which has been encroached upon and built over by urban development, such as an elementary school in the upper left corner. The road has been replaced by a landscaped plaza.

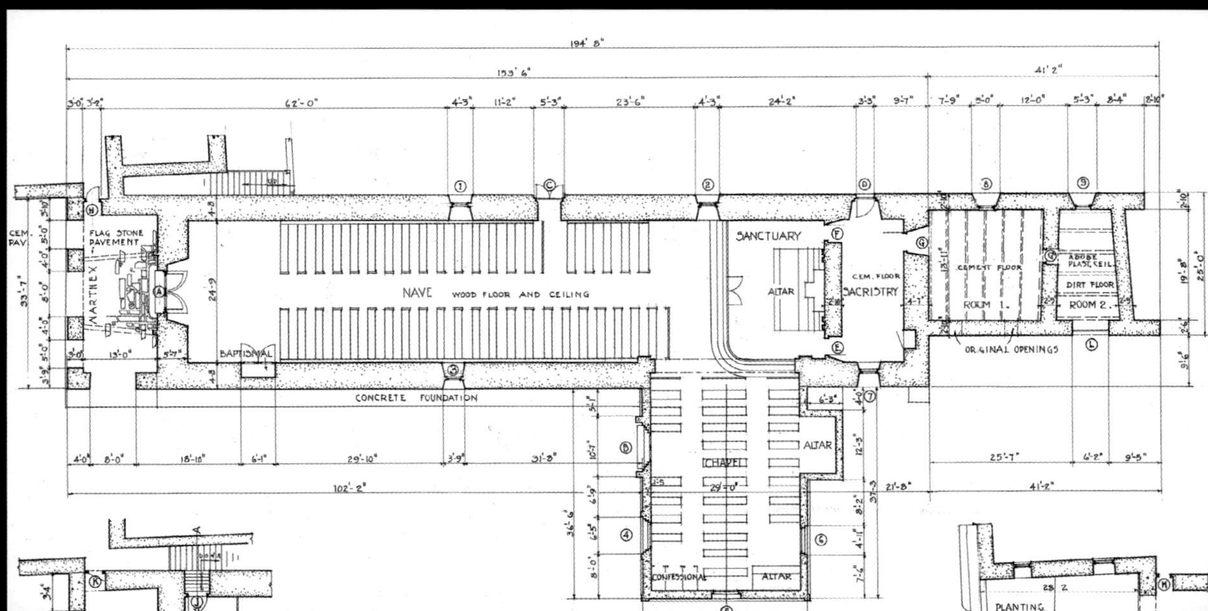

The L-shaped plan is evident, which creates an awkward space where both wings intersect at the altar, breaking the processional integrity of the sanctuary.

These corbels under the choir area are more colorfully Victorian, ornate, and prominent than would be found in the original.

The covered porch and arched portico gives protection to the entry. The church bells have been incorporated into the wall cavity instead of being in a taller tower, which would be more separate from the building.

Wrought iron candelabras are reminiscent of the originals. Note the plank ceiling and decorative corbels in the main space.

San Francisco de Asís, 1776

Mission San Francisco de Asís, 1776

Mission San Francisco de Asís, 1776

The Mission San Francisco de Asís is the sixth mission founded in California. It was founded on June 29, 1776, by Friar Francisco Palou and named for Saint Francis of Assisi, founder of the Franciscan Order.

While Father Serra and Inspector-General Galvez were planning the first three missions in Alta California, Father Serra lamented that there were no plans to name a mission after the founder. He got his chance when after the Portola party missed finding Monterey Bay, they found a great bay, which was so large that they at first didn't realize it was a bay at all, thinking it was the ocean itself.

Soon after, the Viceroy ordered two mission settlements there. Lt. Col. Juan Bautista de Anza led 240 settlers and 1,000 head of cattle to Monterey from Sonora, Mexico, to put down roots. Shortly thereafter he took a smaller party to San Francisco itself, where he selected a site for a presidio and another for the mission. He chose a spot on a bank of a rivulet that he christened Arroyo de los Dolores because it was the feast day of Our Lady of Sorrows, which also became the name of the mission. By October 9th, a wooden church had been erected.

Mission life was not very pleasant for the Native Americans. A severe climate did much with chilling fogs and winds from the sea. Sickness was a major factor in limiting the indigenous population of the mission. Measles epidemics in 1806 and 1826 were responsible for more than 500 Native American deaths. Five thousand and five hundred Native Americans died here during the mission's 58 years of existence. For years, the mission was faced with the problem of neophytes (converted natives) running away to join their friends across the bay. Twenty years after the founding, a group of 14 neophytes sent to search for the runaways was attacked and half were killed.

After secularization in 1834, the mission began to decline. The current picturesque pedimented church was begun in 1782, when Father Palou moved the mission to a more favorable site in its present location. It was dedicated in 1791. Redwood was available for construction from Monterey north. Wooden pegs of manzanita were commonly used to connect timbers in structures. The façade of the building was not built until about 1810, when skilled masons were available in the area. The large quadrangle, of which it was a corner, has been filled in over time while the small church has remained untouched. Spared by the earthquakes of 1906 and 1989, it has been carefully preserved, strengthened when necessary, and faithfully kept in its original state, though it is now in an urban setting.

This unique and dramatic façade is unlike any other mission. It is a modified Greek temple with a whimsical approach to the bells, which is playful and classical, too.

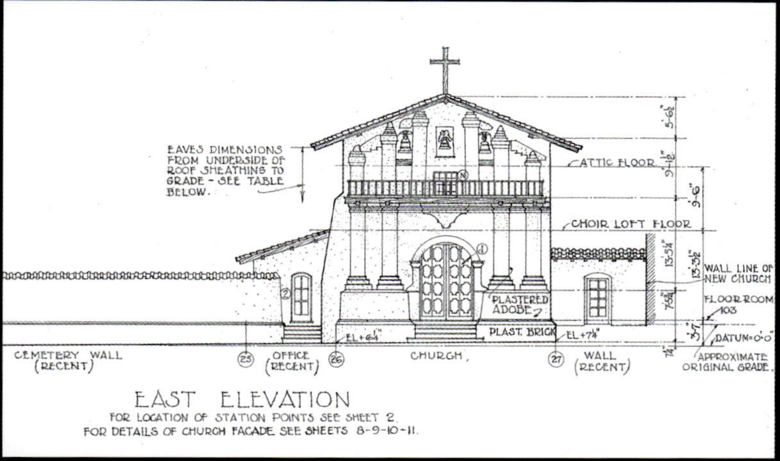

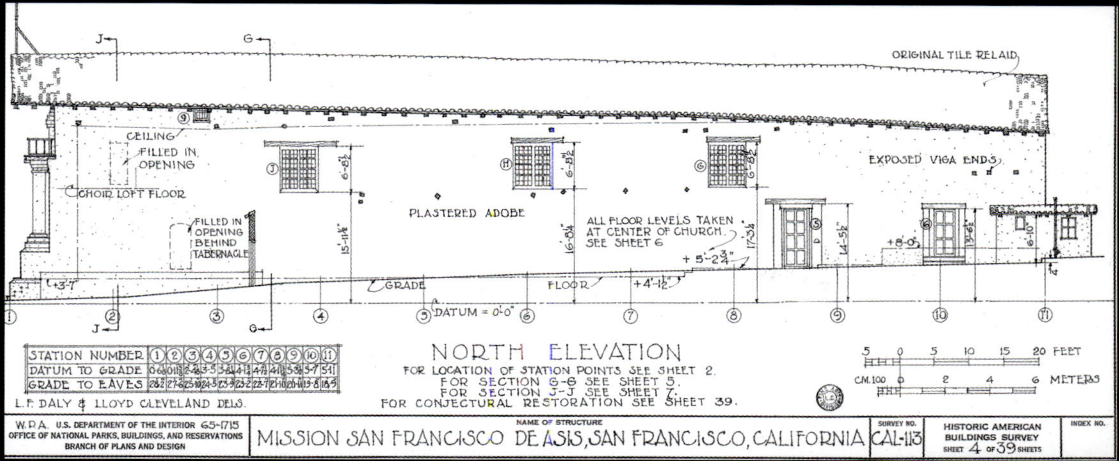

Measured drawings document the classical pedimented entry and heavy relief on the façade.

The mission in its various incarnations, which show the original building in model form, then with the two-story addition, and finally with the massive new church next door that is a survivor with damage from the 1906 earthquake all around.

This is an original *retablo* in gilt with ornate carving, similar to the missions of Yucatan from two centuries earlier. These large and dramatic wooden walls often covered up, and so protected, earlier murals from the Spanish days, which are still being uncovered today.

The altarpiece of the *retablo*.

Painted decoration often was used to replace the more difficult task of carving.

Painted wood and provincial sculpture were used to explain the Bible's saints and stories to many early locals who could not read.

Mission San Juan Capistrano, 1776

Mission San Juan Capistrano, 1776

Mission San Juan Capistrano, 1776

The Mission San Juan Capistrano, named for Saint John of Capistrano, Italy, a fourteenth-century theologian, is the seventh mission founded in California. It was actually founded twice: once on November 1, 1776, by Friar Junípero Serra, but previously by Friar Fermin Lasuén on October 30, 1775, and then abandoned.

In 1775, Father Lasuén set up a cross and dedicated the location. The work went on for eight days until it stopped when word arrived of an attack on the San Diego Mission by Native Americans. The bells were buried and the party returned to San Diego. A year later, Father Serra journeyed to the site and dug up the bells, hung them from a tree and conducted a service on that first day of November. Within a year, the first chapel was built, a very modest structure that is still being used to this day. It is called "Father Serra's Church" because it is one of the few still standing where he is known to have said Mass. (The other is Mission Dolores.)

Almost immediately the mission prospered. The valley was fertile, pleasant, and had a moderate climate. The fields soon yielded abundant harvests and the livestock prospered. A patio was built that was surrounded by shops, storehouses and even barracks for soldiers. The patio was irregular in shape due to the padres measuring by pacing off rather than with a surveyor's instruments.

In 1796, the original chapel had been long outgrown by the population. An expert stonemason arrived from Mexico and he, with many Native Americans, built a cathedral-like church in nine years. It was the most magnificent church in all of the California missions, measuring 180 feet long by 40 feet wide. It was made in the form of a cross and had a vaulted ceiling with seven domes. The main entrance had a bell tower standing 120 feet into the sky and could be seen for nearly ten miles. Four bells were mounted between 1796 and 1804. In 1806, the completion was celebrated with a two-day fiesta with all the civil, military, and religious dignitaries attending.

In December of 1812, just as the bells were ringing for the next Mass, the floor and walls shook as an earthquake hit. The building collapsed, leaving approximately forty bodies to be dug out. The mission soon recovered, but the padres moved back into the original church, rather than rebuild the stone church again. All further construction was limited to utilitarian needs.

In 1833, the Native Americans were emancipated. Unfortunately, they were left subject to the control of the civil administrators who took much of their wealth. By 1844, few Native Americans were left. The mission itself suffered the secularization imposed on it. Plundered of tiles and lumber, the buildings deteriorated quickly. Finally, in the 1890s, the Landmarks Club saved the Serra Church from disintegration. In the 1920s, Father St. John O'Sullivan started a major restoration, laying out gardens and repairing the grounds.

While the famous swallow migration has been spread over the Orange County area, the ruins of the stone church still stand and the remnants of the stonework stand testament to the work that was performed.

This fine model shows the original mission lost in an earthquake. The vaulted spaces are reminiscent of the Morrocan roots of the Spanish friars. The church domes made of stone collapsed and its ruins remain in place today.

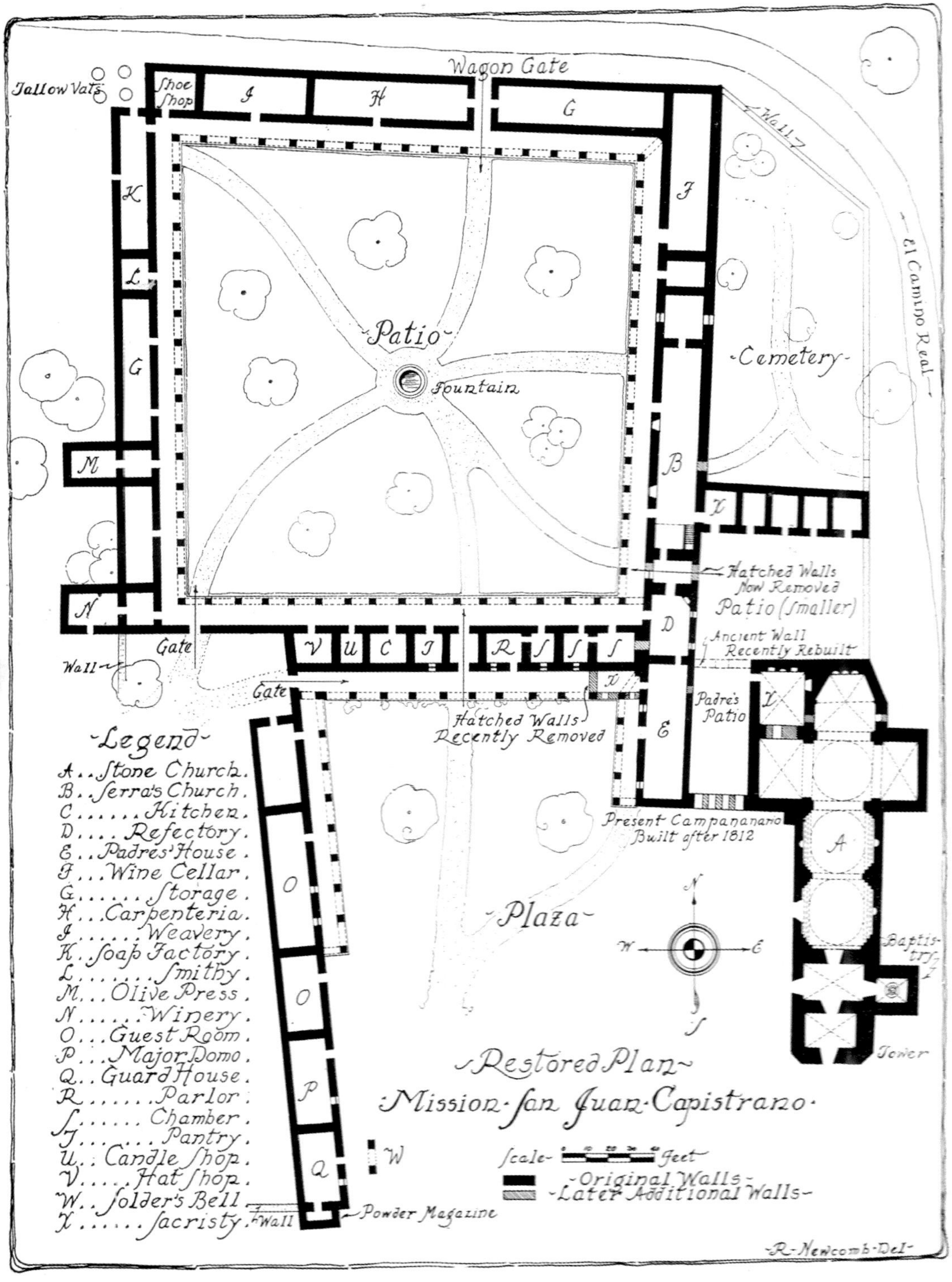

These drawings show the complexity of the mission's site plan, with its many shops and support structures.

The plaza of the quadrangle, with its large fountain, retains the original charm and heart of the mission. The perimeter buildings housed leather, weavers, and candle-makers as well as administrative offices and clergy quarters.

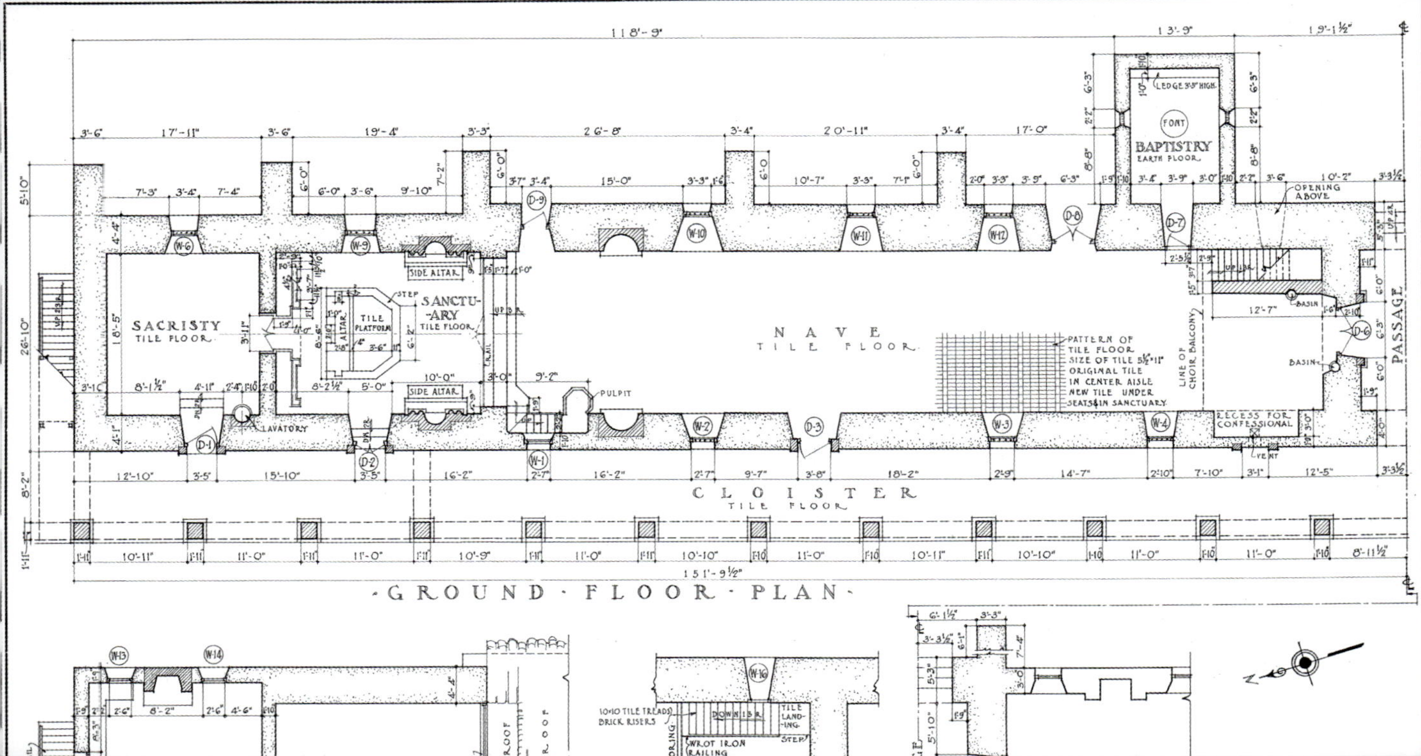
LEDGE 3'-9" HIGH
FONT
BAPTISTRY
EARTH FLOOR
OPENING ABOVE
SIDE ALTAR
STEP
SANCTU-ARY
TILE FLOOR
SACRISTY
TILE FLOOR
TILE PLATFORM
ALTAR
NAVE
TILE FLOOR
PATTERN OF TILE FLOOR
SIZE OF TILE 5½"×11"
ORIGINAL TILE IN CENTER AISLE
NEW TILE UNDER SEATS & IN SANCTUARY
LINE OF CHOIR BALCONY
BASIN
PASSAGE
PULPIT
LAVATORY
RECESS FOR CONFESSIONAL
VENT
CLOISTER
TILE FLOOR
GROUND · FLOOR · PLAN
10×10 TILE TREADS
BRICK RISERS
DOWN 13 R.
TILE LANDING
WROT IRON RAILING

Father Serra's Chapel on the grounds is one of the oldest structures in California. Its intimate richness attests to the veneration of the padre. This *reredos* installed in the 1920s, with its painted surfaces and grand pulpit, inspires a sense of awe in the congregation. One of the oldest buildings in California, it is one of the few where Father Serra served Mass.

This is a different view of the same chapel, looking away from the altar toward the choir and entry.

The pulpit is raised and highly carved. A window is beautifully placed to light the way to the lectern.

An imported altarpiece with gilt and carved wood, which shows the skill and the care lavished on the church's Serra Chapel interior.

While the colors are a little too strong in this restoration, these painted Native American patterns create a sumptuous setting at a very low cost. The patterns are said to be similar to examples found in Native American, pre-mission design motifs.

This is the chapel-side courtyard, which sits behind the horizontal bell tower wall. Its raw ranchero appearance and character are very close to the way missions existed at their peak, the very productive period from 1800–1822.

This image is a south facing view of the same court showing a *campanario*, a wall pierced with bells, with an unusual horizontal layout.

These unique door frames of stone and Native American-inspired moldings show the importance given to this mission, which is one of only three stone missions. The artistic intent and quality of the details shows the padres' higher aspirations for San Juan Capistrano.

Deep set, grilled, and in a variety of shapes, these windows provide a sense of security and a luminous glow to the interior spaces.

Ingenious chimney stacks were another way to give the buildings design interest. The simple terracotta tile caps served the functional purpose of shedding rain.

Wrought iron gates provide security and decoration for the missions passageways. It served the function of being durable yet impenetrable.

Mission Santa Clara de Asís, 1777

Mission Santa Clara de Asís, 1777

Mission Santa Clara de Asís, 1777

The Mission Santa Clara de Asís is the eighth mission founded in California. It was founded on January 12, 1777, by Friar Junípero Serra. Santa Clara was the second of the San Francisco missions, which were placed per the Viceroy's order that two settlements were to be near the great port to prevent enemy occupation or attack.

The first, Mission Dolores, had been established in 1776, and everyone was ready for the second mission to be founded, but authorization was delayed due to Native American uprisings in San Luis Obispo. Eventually, the building was begun at a site about forty miles southeast of Mission Dolores, on the bank of a stream named Rio de Nuestra Señora de Guadalupe by Juan Bautista de Anza.

On January 5, 1777, they then laid out the square with space for the church, dwellings, granaries, and a guardhouse. The buildings started soon after. Unfortunately, the indigenous population came to conflict with the soldiers after killing some of the soldiers' mules and a detachment was sent from San Francisco. Finding Native Americans feasting on the mule meat, the soldiers attempted to capture them. The prisoners were taken to Santa Clara and there flogged. The Native Americans continued to steal from the mission. In May, an epidemic struck, killing many of the indigenous children. Also, Santa Clara had problems with the nearby Pueblo of San Jose, which was founded the same year as Santa Clara. The settler's cattle frequently mixed with the mission's, and there were heated disputes of water rights to the Guadalupe River.

Due to flooding, the buildings had to be moved several times. In 1781, the cornerstone was laid for a new church, the third, as per the designs of Father Murguia. Father Serra arrived and blessed the cross and the cornerstone. Less than four months later Father Serra died. In 1911, the cornerstone was found during some sitework. In it were found small crucifixes and Spanish coins, which are now on display in the museum.

In 1836, when the secularization took place, the Native Americans were dispersed and the land occupied. Later, the land was partly returned to the Church, which gave the site to the Jesuit Order for use as a college seat. In 1851, classes began and the college that is now the University of Santa Clara was chartered by the state four years later.

In 1926, a fire burned the church to the ground. It was rebuilt and enlarged in 1929.

The structure was rebuilt and enlarged in the 1930s. Unfortunately, it lacks the rustic charm of the original building.

Mission San Buenaventura, 1782

Mission San Buenaventura, 1782

Mission San Buenaventura, 1782

The Mission San Buenaventura is the ninth mission founded in California. Originally planned to be the third mission, it was founded on March 31, 1782, by Friar Junípero Serra and named for Saint Bonaventure, who was born near Viterbo, Italy, in 1221.

San Buenaventura was delayed by twelve years due to problems at other missions, which required the military forces necessary to defend a new mission.

In March of 1782, eight soldiers and their families rode for the new mission location with cattle and pack animals loaded with church goods, furnishings, and tools. Included in the group was Governor Neve, who was personally guarded by ten soldiers. The mission was located at a Native American town of 500 people named La Asuncion de Nuestra Señora by Father Crespi. On Easter Sunday morning, Father Serra officially founded the mission by performing Mass. This was the last mission Father Serra founded personally.

The building of the local chapel proceeded immediately. The Native Americans helped with the building for payment, but they resisted joining the life of the mission. Sometime in the next ten years the mission church burned and a new larger one of stone was begun. In 1809, the new church was dedicated, but three years later the violent earthquake of 1812 severely damaged the mission. The next year saw the repairs completed and a reinforcement of the church by the addition of an immense buttress.

In 1818, the Mojave tribe came to trade. The soldiers objected and locked them up. In the morning, a fight erupted, resulting in twelve deaths. From that day forward, the Mojaves did what they could to thwart the work of the mission.

1782

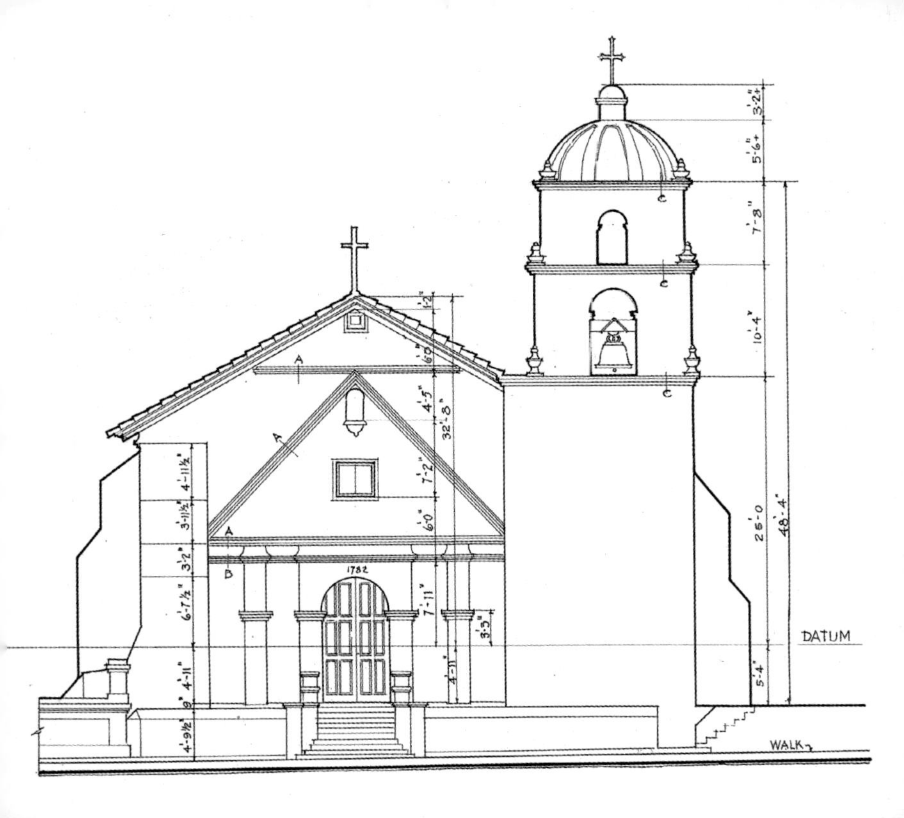

This HABS measured drawing is useful in studying the proportions for the actual structure. The three-step domed tower is the same as those used on four of the different missions. It has also been copied in many new buildings as the essential characteristic feature of the mission style.

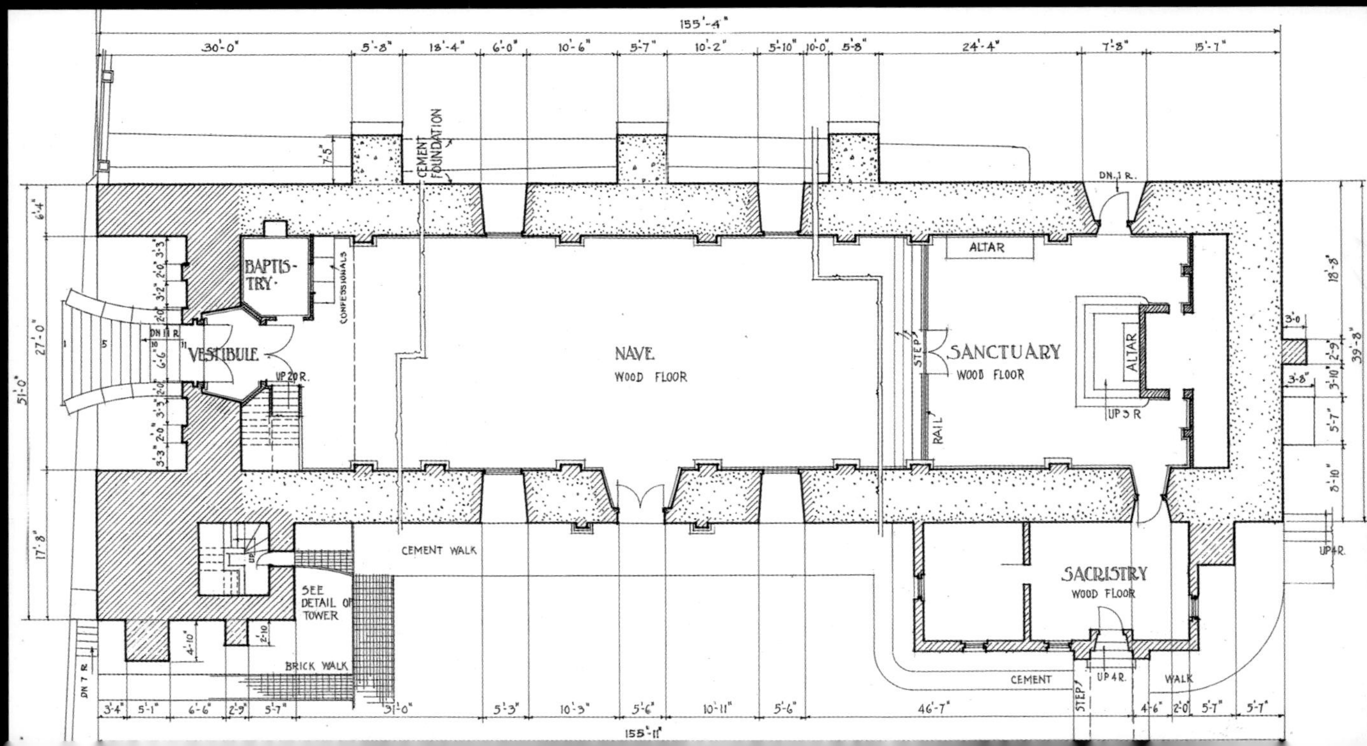

This model shows the extensive original mission site, which has been whittled down and hemmed in by urban development in the city of Ventura—it was originally out in the open countryside.

Swags and plasterwork are used to decorate the plain walls and festive bell tower.

The interior has heavy Victorian elements that look strong and rich but are not really of the Mission era.
A few details like those on the following page harken back to its original simple elegance.

Mission Santa Barbara, 1786

Mission Santa Bárbara Virgen y Martir, 1786

Mission Santa Bárbara Virgen y Martir 1786

The Mission Santa Barbara is the tenth mission founded in California. It was founded on December 4, 1786, by Friar Fermin Lasuén and is known as the "Queen of the Missions" because of its great architectural presence. Santa Barbara is the only mission in the California chain that has remained under the control of the Franciscans without interruption, from the day of its founding until the present.

Santa Barbara got off to a delayed start when the governor decided he would not authorize additional missions for Father Serra because he opposed the expansion of the mission system. He felt it gave the padres too much economic power. Father Serra accompanied the governor to the presidio location at Santa Barbara but he did not realize the governor had already persuaded the viceroy to withhold funds for a separate mission.

Father Serra blessed the location of the presidio and performed Mass, then waited there for nearly three weeks before the governor told Father Serra that the mission would not be approved until the presidio was completed. Sadly, Father Serra departed for Carmel. He visited the presidio twice the next year but died before approval was finally granted.

Father Fermin Francisco de Lasuén, the successor to Father Serra, thus founded Mission Santa Barbara. On December 4, 1786, the site was dedicated at a place called the *El Pedregoso* ("Rocky Mound"). It was a grand plan.

The buildings were made of logs, topped by beams covered with reeds, and then made of mud and thatch. Later, an adobe wing was added and more buildings until the standard quadrangle was eventually completed. Approximately 250 native homes were built in rows to the left of the mission. A water system was completed along with a tannery, pottery, and more warehouses. In 1808, a Moorish fountain was built, surrounded by some pepper trees.

As the mission grew, three churches were built, each larger than the one before. In 1812, a large earthquake almost completely destroyed the last one. It was repaired and used for several years while a new, bigger stone church was built around it. This church, the one that stands today, was dedicated in September of 1820 after five years of construction. In 1925, another earthquake damaged this church and, fortunately, California paid for the repairs this time. But in 1950, cracks started to appear in the façade. The concrete used in 1925 had weakened the front of the church and it had to be rebuilt using steel-reinforced concrete. The new stone facing still retains the original appearance. The pedimented façade is patterned after the Pantheon in Rome. The design has been traced to a book brought to California by the Franciscans, a Spanish reprint of an architecture book originally published in 27 B.C. by Vitruvius.

The mission was quite successful in its agricultural pursuits. This was due in large part to a water system so sophisticated that parts of it are still in use today in the city of Santa Barbara. A stone aqueduct system channeled water from a stream two miles away to a large holding tank near the mission. Some water was even sent through a filtration system to make it suitable for drinking.

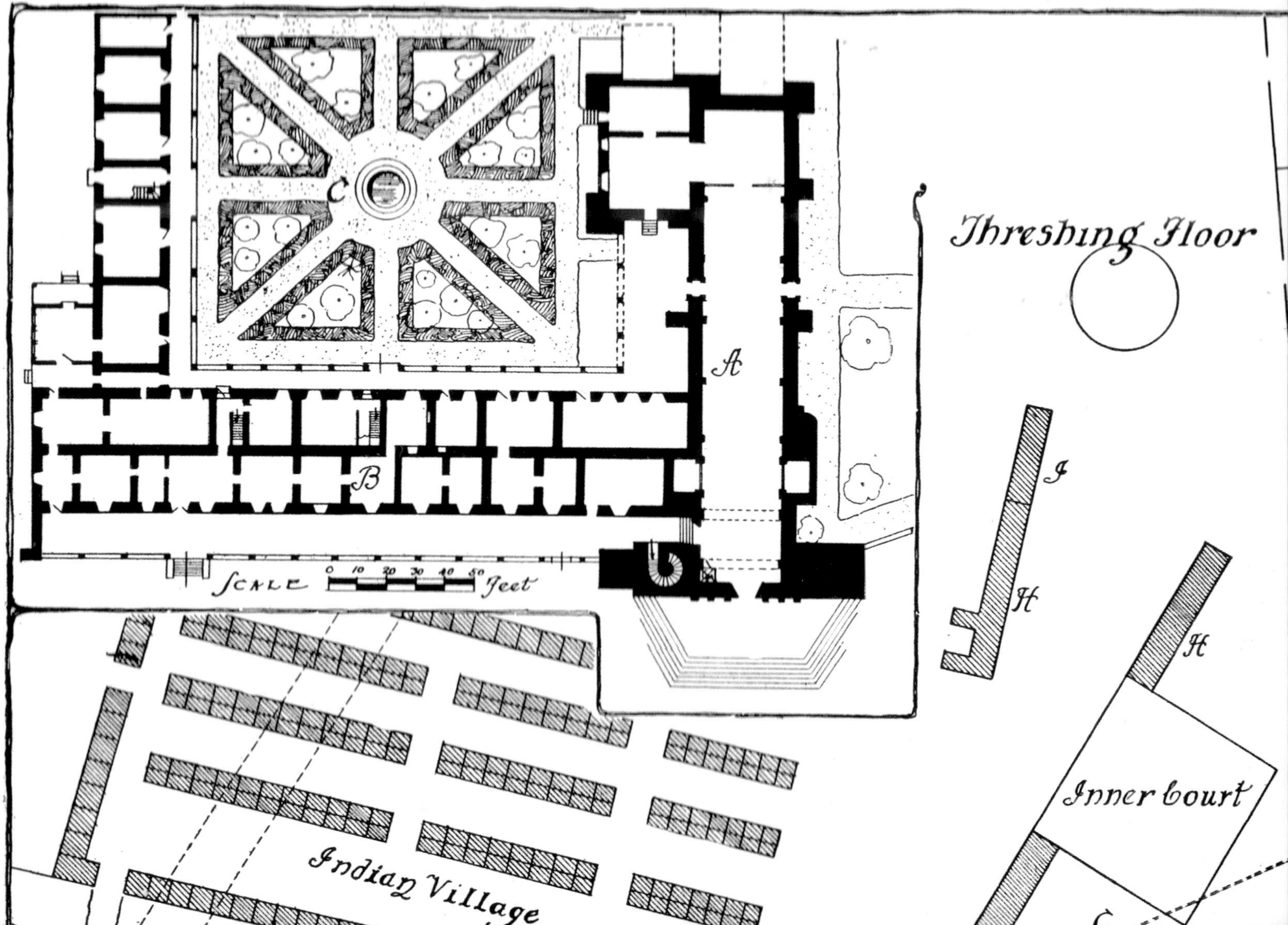

This site plan of the mission shows the quadrangle, convent, sanctuary, and early Native American village.

The model shows how the building looked in its final form.

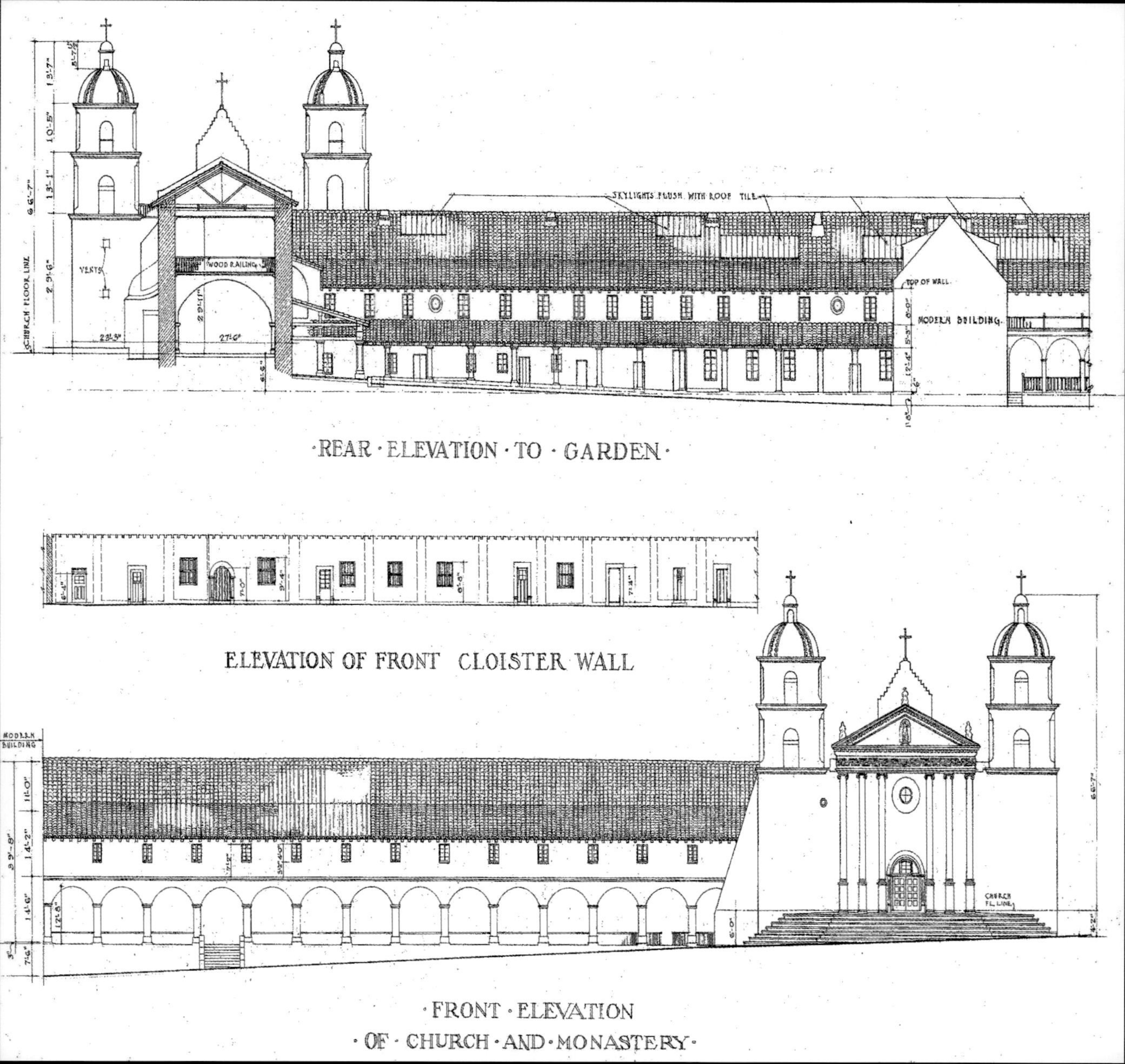

These HABS measured drawings of the Santa Barbara Mission show the south facing 1812 pedimented façade. The model (opposite) and the plan drawing show the broadside view of the building from the east.

Model of the mission showing a cut-away roof and a view from a raised angle, highlighting the strong buttressing on the cemetery side.

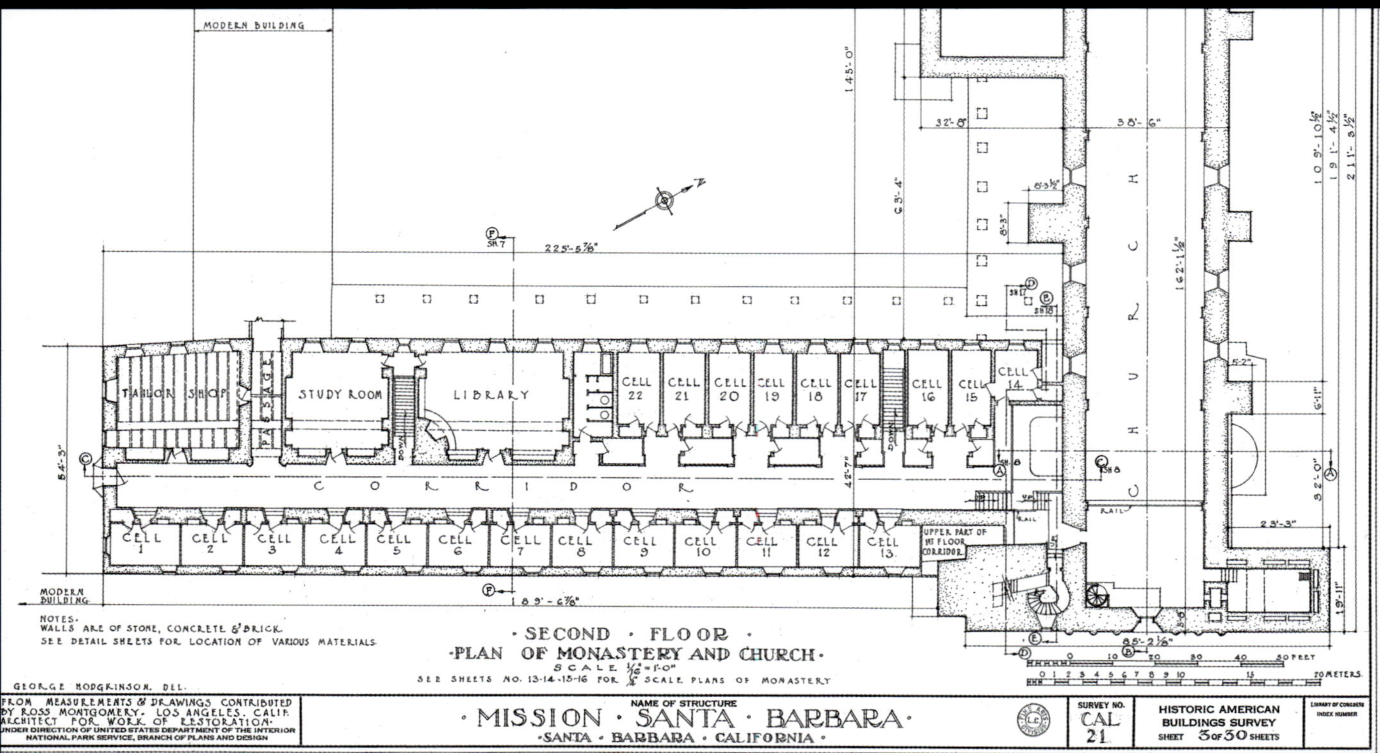

The HABS measured plans of the monastery wing and church sanctuary, at right, about 1812.

The mission's repair and restoration of 1825 remained true to the beloved original pre-earthquake style.

View of the altar and the main sanctuary. The cemetery entrance is midway down the aisle on the right.

Choir view and baptistery in the main aisle, which is very similar to that of San Luis Rey. The round window above the entry was covered on the inside until recently, but is now being reopened as a solstice window.

West elevation of the main church sanctuary, seen from the inside of the main quadrangle.

Same quadrangle looking to the northwest, with a view of the convent and clergy quarters.

Two mission porch arcades, one built of plaster and block (at the entry) and one in dressed stone (off the courtyard).

A beautifully plaster-scalloped, rustic portal to the cemetery from the sanctuary.

This is the same doorway but looking from the cemetery (outside) into and through the church.

Architectural details on the doors, ceilings, and grillwork, so vital in creating the style and character of the mission.

Lighting fixtures showing the style and variety at the mission

Front door wrought iron hardware at the main entry to the mission.

Wrought iron grillwork and candlesticks.

Decorative railings and wrought iron lighting embellish the bare walls of the mission.

This close-up of the railing and wall attachment show the level of artistic detail found in the mission.

This graceful stairway incorporates the iron handrail—each picket is attached individually and directly to the adobe wall.

Mission of La Purísima Concepción de Maria Santísima, 1787

Mission La Purísima Concepción de Maria Santísima, 1787

Mission La Purísima Concepción de Maria Santísima, 1787

The Mission La Purísima Concepción de Maria Santísima is the eleventh mission founded in California. It was founded on December 8, 1787, by Friar Fermin Lasuén.

In March of 1788, soldiers and workmen arrived to start building, delayed by the rainy season. In early April, Father Lasuén arrived with two padres to take charge. In only four months, they had baptized seventy-five Native Americans. Within three years the mission was doing very well. The first building fell into ruins since it was hastily built. New facilities were completed in 1802, built of adobe and roofed in tile. The mission had a good period of productivity that was shattered when the earthquake of 1812 hit on the morning of December 21. The church was badly damaged and a second quake collapsed most of the buildings.

Construction of a new mission was begun, and Native Americans worked to complete the buildings. Earthquake resistance was designed into these new buildings and as such it is the only mission complex not built in a quadrangle. Eventually, the mission prospered with large herds, warehouses, a mill, a blacksmith shop, bakeries, and other shops.

In 1816, a drought came to the area and many sheep died; in 1818, a fire swept through, burning many of the homes. Since Mexico declared independence in 1821, the missions had been on their own with no supplies and no pay for the soldiers. Revolt soon followed since the Native Americans became restless under the acts of the soldiers. In 1824, at Mission Santa Inés, a guard flogged a Native American. The indigenous people attacked the soldiers and two Native Americans died amid great destruction of the mission. When the Native Americans at La Purísima heard of the news, they seized the mission.

They fortified the grounds and mounted two old cannons. They held the mission for nearly a month, until soldiers from Monterey arrived and took the mission. Sixteen Native Americans and a few soldiers died. Seven Native Americans were condemned to death and eighteen others were imprisoned.

Soon after this fight, secularization arrived and Mission Purisima collapsed into ruin. In 1845, the land and treasures were sold to the Don Juan Temple of Los Angeles for $1,100. In 1933, the Union Oil Company donated the mission property and the surrounding area to the public. This area is now a 966-acre state historic park. The National Park Service and the C.C.C. started reconstruction. In 1934, only a few fragments of walls were left and in 1951, the entire mission was rebuilt using original tools and methods wherever possible. The mission was then turned over to the state to administer as a Historic Park. Ten fully restored buildings, with 37 furnished rooms, can now be seen as they originally appeared. It is by far the most well-preserved and reconstructed of the mission complexes, in the most natural setting.

The mission has changed little from the original, thanks to a fine and sensitive restoration.

The only linear plan for any mission is that of La Purísima. There is no courtyard. It is laid out along a low slope and stretches in a line in a series of rooms and walled patios. Of all the missions this one has the most pristine and original setting.

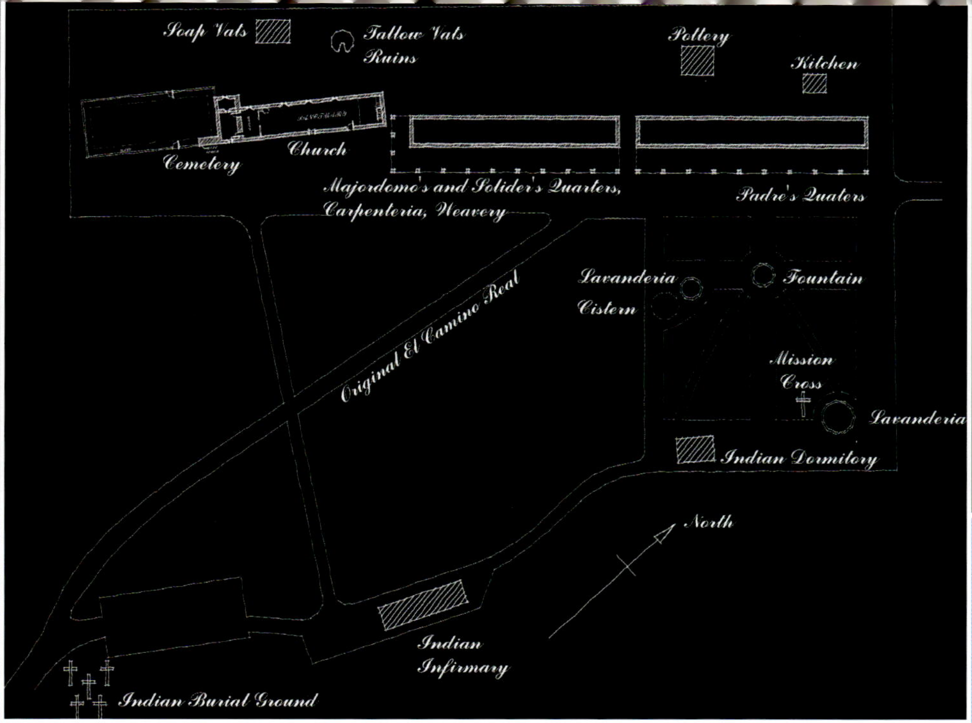

Each of the buildings houses a chapel of extraordinary beauty. Dark and mysterious, they harken back to the Moroccan bazaars with hanging fixtures and frescoed walls, and beautifully decorated altars.

Even cathedrals in Spain would have a hard time matching the elegance of these simple shapes laid out with a great sense of proportion, propriety, and good design.

The Padre's Chapel in the east building wing of the mission is worth a visit in itself to experience the proportions and serenity of the space. Rustic floorboards and colorful but tasteful window and wall trim fill the space with delight.

With almost no actual detail, the faux painted walls and deep-set windows create an atmosphere of serene peace. These are the raw essentials of architecture put to work to create a sum more than its parts. The rustic simplicity feels not only appropriate to the site, but retains a wholesome freshness, like the countryside in which it sits.

Symbolic "River of Life" wood doors, wrought iron hardware, and wood floors provide an elegant feel to a simple space.

Creative architectural elements, like the wood screens and wall-hung pulpit, give the space homespun charm with design interest.

The dramatic play of light and shadow in the deep walls, arranged in a structural pattern, give strength and interest to the whole. Simply painted frames give the room a great deal of colorful flair.

This is the sleeping quarters of the padre, which, though simple with only natural materials, has a rustic charm and warmth characteristic of the style—primitive, restrained, and beautiful.

This room is the mission's main administrative office. The serpentine pattern on the wood door at the left is known as the "River of Life," symbolic of the faith journey. This pattern is found in nearly every mission.

Repetitive patterns and deep walls create the strong simple building elevations, which are powerfully expressive in their simplicity.

This colonnade runs the length of this south facing porch. The sunny notch at each column corner creates a painterly detail, which helps make the setting picturesque, lively, and functional all at once. The spalling plaster and rich patina of the plaster with the eroded adobe only add to the charm.

These images show various details of hardware, trim, window treatments, and recesses which create the rustic handmace anc humanly scaled character of the mission style

An olive grove surrounding a stepped fountain creates a serene country glade.

This rural setting is blessed by nature. La Purísima Mission, above all, plainly shows why the sites were originally chosen for their natural beauty and close resources, the best of the New World coast land.

Mission Santa Cruz, 1791

Mission La Exaltación de la Santa Cruz, 1791

Mission La Exaltación de la Santa Cruz, 1791

The Mission La Exaltación de la Santa Cruz is the twelfth mission founded in California. It was founded on August 28, 1791, by Friar Fermin Lasuén and named for the Sacred Cross.

In 1769, Captain Gaspar de Portola rode through the area and gave it the name Santa Cruz (which is Spanish for "Holy Cross")—a new mission, Santa Cruz. After a 1791 flood, work began on a new, higher site, with a church that had a stone foundation and thick adobe brick walls 112 feet long and 29 feet wide. This was the main church at the mission for 65 years.

The Native Americans who lived and worked at the mission were the local Ohlone people, and early on the number at the mission grew to about 500 people. The trade of the mission began successfully. Crops and orchards soon were thriving in the fertile soil along the San Lorenzo River. Records from 1796 show that the mission produced 1,200 bushels of grain, 600 bushels of corn, and 60 bushels of beans that year.

After six years, the mission began to encounter outside difficulty. In 1797, the governor of Alta California decided that a pueblo (town) should be built directly across the San Lorenzo River from the mission. The priest protested, believing that the town would attract badly behaved citizens. Nevertheless, a pueblo was established on the east side of the river, named Villa de Branciforte. Many of the priest's worst fears came true. Convicted criminals settled in the town, and it soon became the center of low-life crime.

The priests were upset, as some of the neophytes were leaving the mission: some to join this new town, some to escape the strict rules and harsh punishment that often occurred at the mission. Soon the priest ordered that once the natives were baptized, they could not return to their villages—if caught as runaways, they were severely punished. Nonetheless, in 1798 alone, nearly one-fourth of the native population ran away.

Meanwhile, the mission priest had another problem starting within the Native American population, who were contracting European diseases. Thousands of natives died. Many neophytes ran away to try to escape these illnesses and thus the diseases spread back to their villages. Mission Santa Cruz never completely recovered from these early tragedies.

In 1831, after the war of Mexican independence, church-owned land was divided up between the Native Americans who had lived there and the nearby Californios, in a process called secularization. After the new Mexican officials arrived, much of what was supposed to go to the natives at Mission Santa Cruz went to the local ranchers instead. About this time, however, smallpox again spread through the mission. The Native American population dropped from about 300 to 71 people. Within a few years, many natives had given up and sold their property to ranchers, and any natives who tried to remain nearby the mission were soon driven out by settlers.

Soon after the Gold Rush, the United States took over California and made it the thirty-first state. In 1859, President Buchanan returned Mission Santa Cruz and about seventeen surrounding acres to the Catholic Church. Several strong earthquakes hit the area after secularization and ruined the original buildings; remnants were cleared away by a misguided clergyman. A one-third sized replica building is all that remains today, with a few outbuildings marking a sad and ignoble end to the story of the Mission of La Exaltación de la Santa Cruz.

A continuing series of unfortunate events led to its decay and eventual closing and replacement. The original church, which was damaged by a series of earthquakes in the nineteenth century, was taken down. A replica scaled to one-third of the original stands there today as a reminder of the first building to stand in Santa Cruz.

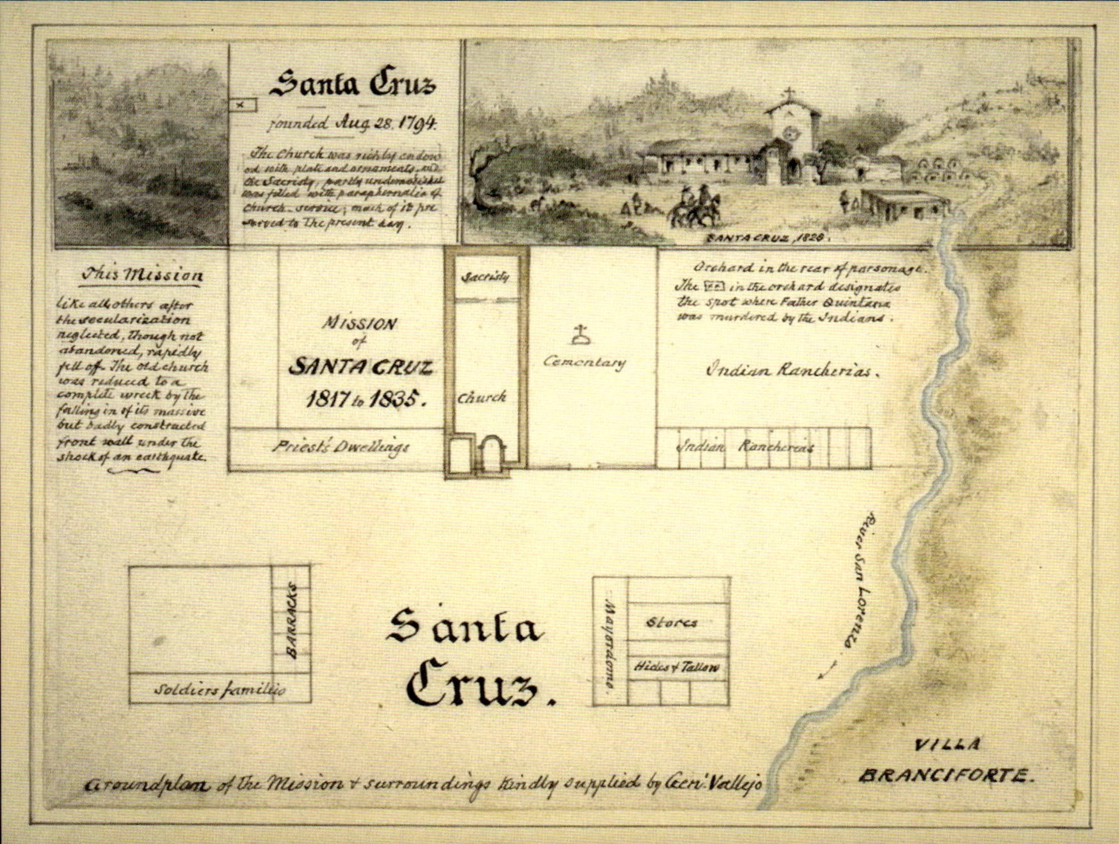

This Borein etching from 1900 shows the original design and setting of the mission, now gone.

Mission Nuestra Señora de la Soledad, 1791

Mission Nuestra Señora de la Soledad, 1791

Mission Nuestra Señora de la Soledad, 1791

The Mission Nuestra Señora de la Soledad is the thirteenth mission founded in California. It was founded on October 9, 1791, by Friar Fermin Lasuén and named for one of the many designations of the Virgin Mary. Located at the site of an Esselen Indian village, a temporary church was constructed in 1791 shortly after its founding, and the first annual report was issued in 1794.

The following years, to 1797, during the administration of the unpopular Padre Diego Garcia, were years of unhappiness at the mission according to historians, since those years coincided with a period of harsh drought conditions, contributing greatly to accusations of deprivation and abuse of the neophytes by Padre Garcia's critics. In 1802, an epidemic and a triple murder contributed to deaths, which for a period of time numbered five or six per day. By 1805, however, the neophyte population had peaked at 688, then slowly dwindled to 598 by 1810.

The secularization inventory in 1836 reported mission property consisting of a vineyard of 5,000 vines; ranchos at San Lorenzo, San Vicente, and San Fernando; and livestock of 3,246 cattle, 2,400 sheep, and 32 horses. Mission liquid assets consisted of $556, while debits amounted to $677. The neophyte population in 1837 was reported at 172, including 45 able-bodied males. In 1839, inspectors found 78 neophytes, with 45 cattle, 685 sheep, 25 horses, and 2 mules. The neophytes complained of grievous wrongdoings by administrators. In 1841, the mission was reported to be in ruins with its vineyards, orchards, and gardens gone wild. The mission buildings, furniture, gardens, and 21 fruit trees, together with one league of land on which resided 20 Native Americans, were sold into private homes. Recent excavations outlining the extent and original configuration of the mission and outbuildings have been completed to document the site.

An early Vischer painting and a current photo of today's mission setting show virtually no change since it was first established.

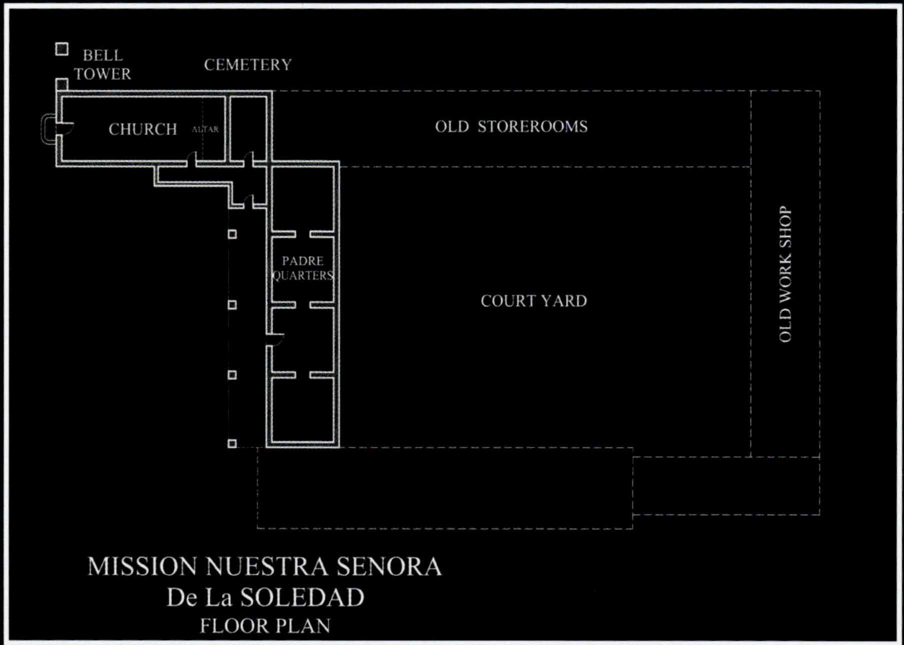

The simple altar and colorful interior create a warm sense of place with the barest of resources.

This colorful ceiling shows that design and creative flair are not limited to a big budget. The graphics also show the Native American's bold imagination and fearless approach to decorative color.

Different wood patterns give the doors variety and interest.

Simple beams and covered porches retain the integrity of the original style.

Internal spaces are lined up wall-to-wall and on a central axis with no hallways. The outside covered porch would be used for access.

Mission San José, 1797

Mission del Gloriosísimo Patriarca San José, 1797

Mission del Gloriosísimo Patriarca San José, 1797

The Mission del Gloriosísimo Patriarca San José is the fourteenth mission founded in California. It was founded on June 11 1797, by Friar Fermin Lasuén.

The work on the site of Mission San José commenced in May 1797 by Native Americans from Mission Santa Clara, 13 miles to the south, under direction of Franciscan missionaries and secular Hispanic overseers. By the end of 1800 the neophyte population had risen to 277, including both Ohlone and Bay Miwok speakers. By the end of 1805, all Native Americans of the East Bay south of Carquinez Strait were at the missions. After a devastating measles epidemic that reduced the mission population by one quarter in 1806, people from more distant areas and new language groups began to join the Mission San Jose community.

The mission's first permanent adobe church was dedicated with great ceremony on April 22, 1809. Valuable gifts of vestments sacred vessels, religious statues, and paintings attested to the generosity of friends of the mission in the Bay Area and abroad. The majority of vestments in the modern collection date from the late eighteenth and early nineteenth centuries. Thousands of cattle roamed the mission ranges, and acres of wheat and other crops were planted and harvested under the direction of the padres In 1868, it produced 4,070 bushels (110 metric tons) of wheat and much produce, including grapes, olives, and figs. In 1832, the mission's 12,000 cattle, 13,000 horses, and 12,000 sheep roamed mission lands from present-day Oakland to San José.

San José was one of the most prosperous of all of the California missions. This prosperity was not to last long, however. On August 17 of that year, the Mexican Congress passed An Act for the Secularization of the Missions of California. During the transition to full secularization, José de Jesús Vallejo (brother of General Mariano G. Vallejo) was appointed civil administrator The mission lands were gradually parceled out to private landowners. The native people fled but found themselves unable to readjust to their former way of life; many subsequently died of disease and starvation. The mission buildings, granaries, orchards and gardens were allowed to decay, and the great herds scattered. Mexican Governor Pío Pico sold the mission property to private interests in 1845 for $12,000. During the 1848 California Gold Rush, H.C. Smith converted the mission to a general store, saloon and hotel.

On October 21, 1868, a 7.0 magnitude earthquake on the Hayward fault, which runs through the grounds of the mission, shattered the walls of the mission church and broke open the roof. The site was cleared and a wood-framed, Gothic-style church was erected directly over the original red-tiled mission floor. In 1890, a Victorian-style rectory was built over the site of a portion of the adobe wing.

Plans to reconstruct the church of Mission San José were launched in 1973. The Victorian-style rectory was relocated to nearby Anza Street and the Gothic-style wooden church was moved to San Mateo where it has been restored as a house of worship by an Anglican church group. After extensive archaeological excavations and planning, construction began in 1982 on a replica of the 1809 adobe church. Work was completed and the facility rededicated on June 11, 1985.

The principal elevation of San José Mission is a classic simple gable with side bell tower, which is the most characteristic façade of the mission style.

An 1876 Vischer painting showing the mission in its native state.

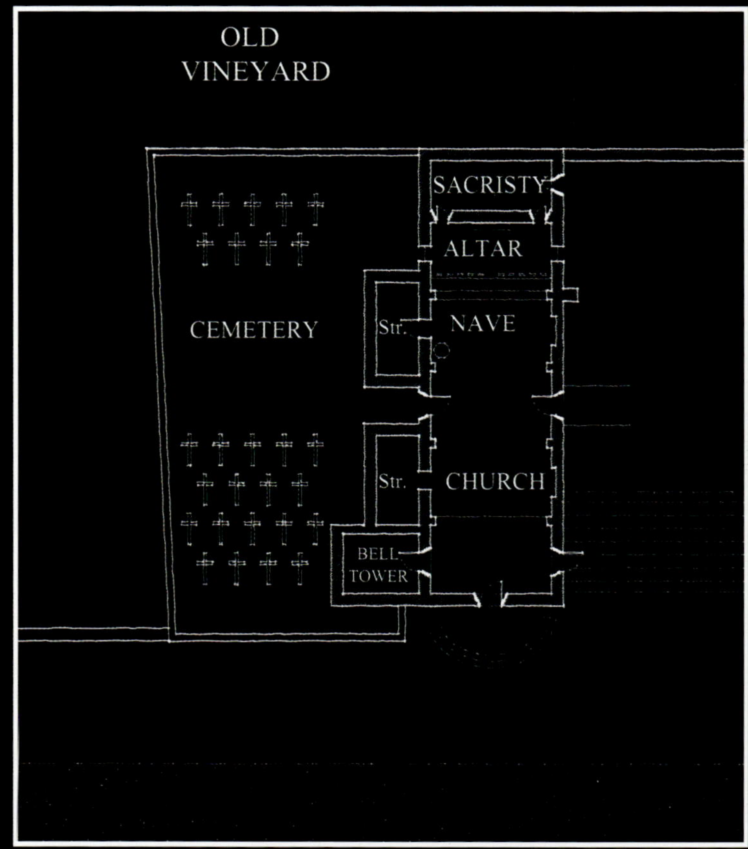

This Carleton Watkins photo, c. 1906, offers another view of the same south-facing elevation in its state of further disrepair, now surrounded with additional construction.

This beautifully restored nave is a large single hall with an *ochovado* ceiling. The symmetry and detail of the altar, along with the side lights at the front of the sanctuary, create a dramatic and lively surprise upon entry. The two walls are faux finished with pediments and swags that give the walls the illusion of depth.

This is a view of the entry and choir loft, organ, and upper window, which is flooding the roof volume with light.

This is the original baptistery for the church.

This stained-wood entry has a grand pediment, is beautifully built, and has unusually good carpentry with a detailed colonial feel.

Deep-set walls provide a solid character for the building; the rough wall texture gives it a rustic air.

Leather thongs for strapping and rustic beams with thatched understacking on the eaves show the natural charm of pioneer rustication, and attests to the scarcity of nails.

Mission San Juan Bautista, 1797

Mission San Juan Bautista, 1797

Mission San Juan Bautista, 1797

The Mission San Juan Bautista is the fifteenth mission founded in California. It was founded on June 24, 1797, by Friar Fermin Lasuén and named for John the Baptist. It is the only church with side aisles joining the nave.

Mission San Juan Bautista's location was selected weeks after founding the Mission San Jose. The mission grew quickly and the Native Americans were so willing to assist that in only six months, they had built an adobe church, granary, barracks, a monastery, and even adobe homes. Soon, however, while the padres considered building either a new church or enlarging the existing one, a series of earthquakes collapsed the existing church. The padres decided to rebuild and enlarge it.

On June 13, 1803, the cornerstone of a new church was laid. This church was designed so that instead of the customary long narrow nave and center aisle, a wider edifice with a nave and side aisles should be erected, with three aisles and a capacity for more than a thousand people. This church was dedicated on June 23, 1812. Fear of earthquakes was justified since the church was built on the edge of the San Andreas fault, yet the mission has stood for more than 200 years, while other buildings have not survived. In 1906, when the big earthquake hit, a few walls fell but there was no major damage. The church was repaired with steel and concrete, combined with some cross-bracing, and is now much stronger.

The interior design of the church continued through 1817, when the floor was tiled and Thomas Doak completed the dramatic painting on the main altar and *reredos*. The church graphics are newly updated and add a great deal of atmosphere to an already beautiful space.

To the north of the church is a peaceful cemetery bordered by one of the few remaining parts of the original El Camino Reál, the first road of California. This cemetery contains the remains of more than 4,000 Christian Native Americans and Europeans. In 1835, the mission was secularized and much of the mission property was seized by the Mexican government. In 1895, the present mission buildings and 55 acres were given back to the Church by the United States government.

As early as 1814, a town grew up around the mission, and while the area surrounding the mission is now a state monument, the church itself has remained and is still active, serving the mostly Spanish-speaking parish. San Juan Bautista has the only original Spanish plaza remaining in California.

The three-arched front elevation reflects the plan inside, with side aisle arcades lining the main sanctuary. San Juan Bautista is the only mission to have side aisles. The bell tower, with its *espadana*-like profile, is a unique and lively element with a European flair.

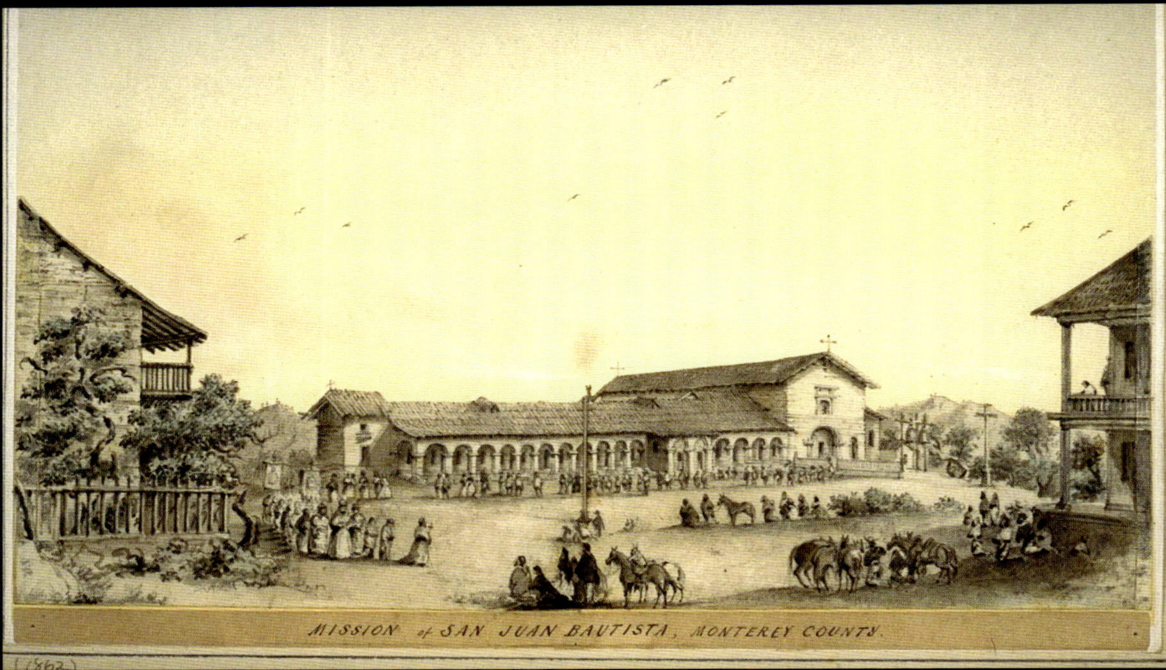

Early church images show the evolution of the entry tower.

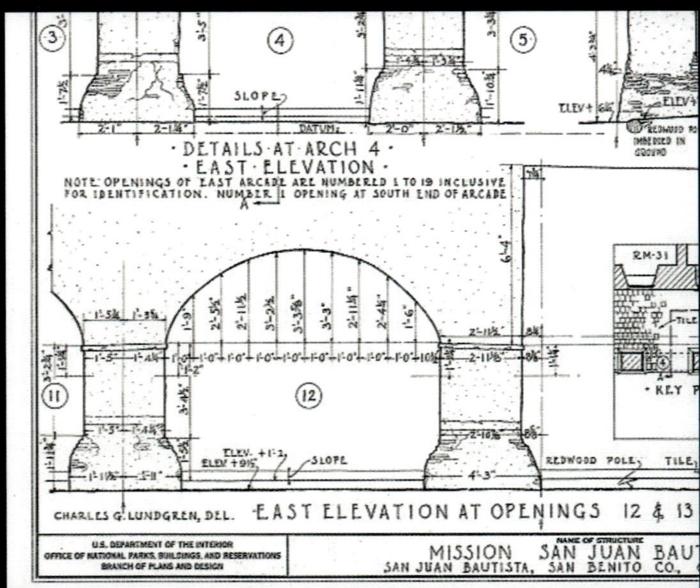
SLOPE
DATUM
DETAILS AT ARCH 4
EAST ELEVATION
NOTE: OPENINGS OF EAST ARCADE ARE NUMBERED 1 TO 19 INCLUSIVE FOR IDENTIFICATION. NUMBER 1 OPENING AT SOUTH END OF ARCADE
RM-31
REDWOOD POLE
CHARLES G. LUNDGREN, DEL.
EAST ELEVATION AT OPENINGS 12 & 13
U.S. DEPARTMENT OF THE INTERIOR
OFFICE OF NATIONAL PARKS, BUILDINGS, AND RESERVATIONS
BRANCH OF PLANS AND DESIGN
NAME OF STRUCTURE
MISSION SAN JUAN BAUT
SAN JUAN BAUTISTA, SAN BENITO CO.

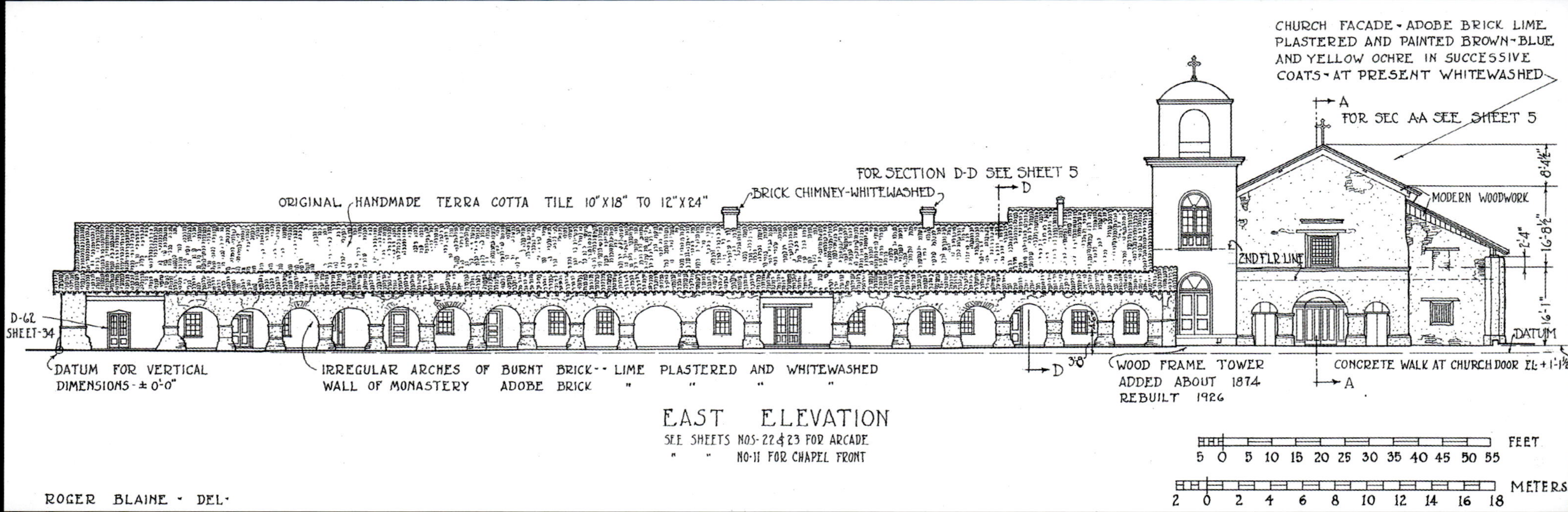

This long arcade shows the mission roots dating back to the Roman aqueducts of the second century. The HABS measured drawing shows the detail.

This long arcade is one of the widest in any of the missions. It is shown in detail here along with the actual photos and the measured drawings of the elevation of a typical bay. It fronts onto a broad park-like lawn showcasing the scope and beauty of the plaza and building. The distant view showcases the long arcade and gives the mission an Old West setting.

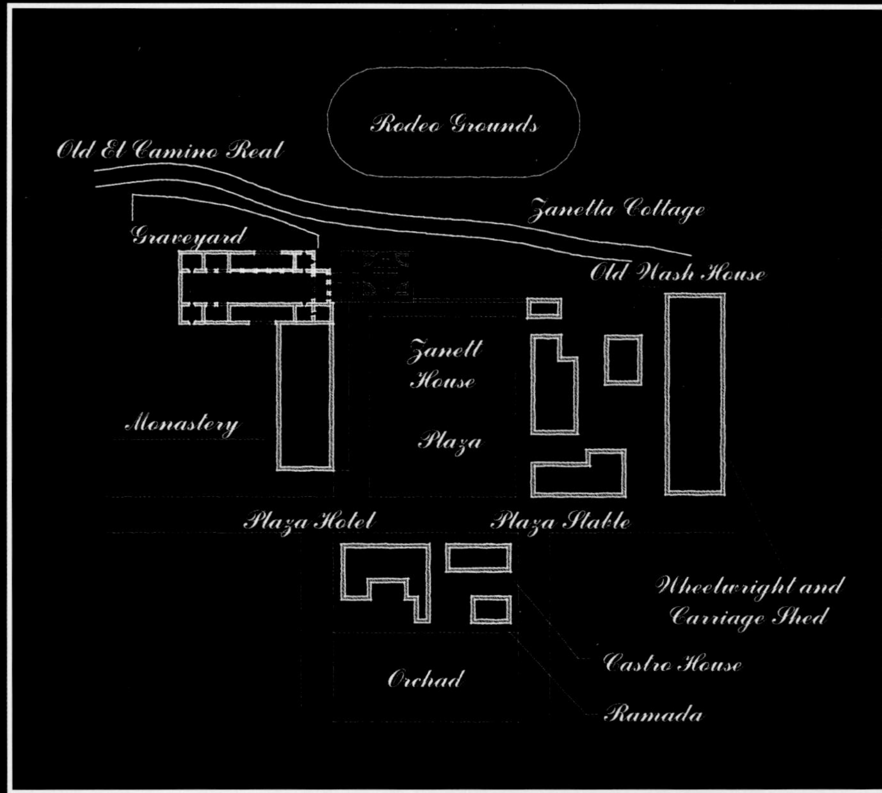

This floor plan is the only cruciform plan of the missions. It gives the interior a sweeping, broad, and mysterious atmosphere by filtering the side light through arcades in the nave walls. The plaza is protected as a landmark now in its original open form.

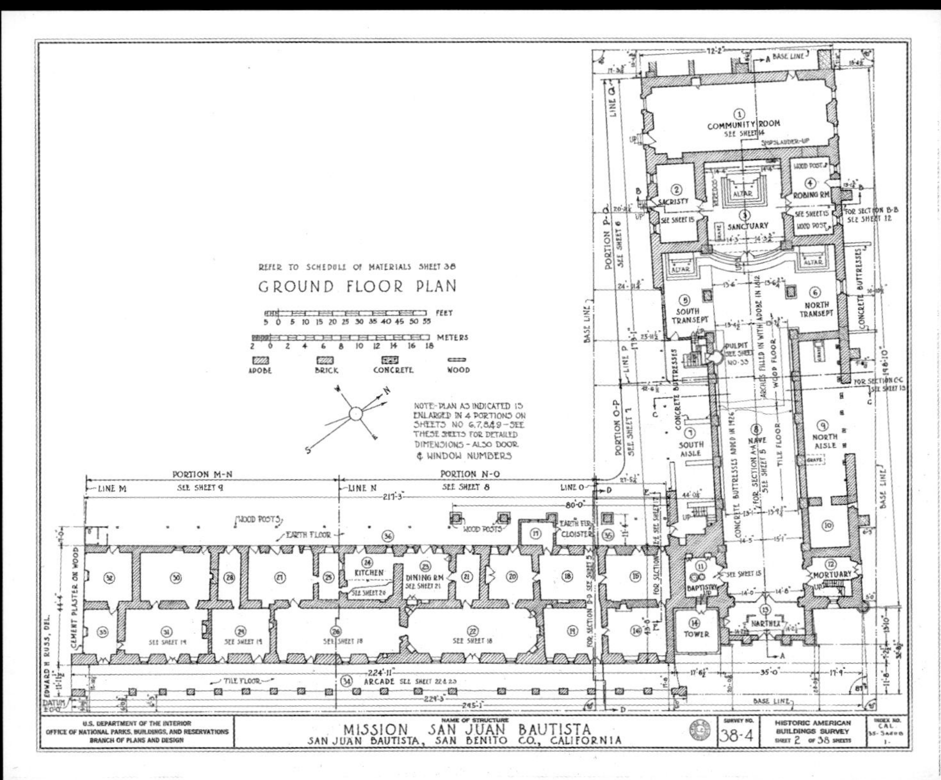

This interior is a cathedral-like adaptation of the *retablos* concept of stacked niches, each with a colorful statue, along with the Native American decorative graphics of a Mexican artisan and a Boston sailor. The

The choir and tall proportions of the space with the side arcades, instead of

Architectural forms are created inside the sanctuary with arcaded walls; the chapel attaches smoothly to the main space and elements like the pulpit are integrated to the overall design, not just attached to a wall.

These rustic but solid rooms show the original rough-hewn character of the spaces.

Simple wall recesses and the sturdy stair approach to the pulpit make the most of what could be standard elements. The stair has a doorway at the top leading into the main space pulpit, from which the padre addresses the congregation.

With soft colors adding to the warmth and atmosphere of the whole, the quiet beauty of the material shines through.

Deep walls with scalloped openings give the doorway a dramatic pattern; they are built in elegance at very little cost.

These reproductions of period wrought-iron candelabras not only show the artisans' talent but also add to the delicacy of the setting.

The simple cadence of the pilasters, open beams, and patterned floor tiles gives the mission a human scale, which makes them inviting, hospitable, and universally admired.

A favorite design motif in missions was a door flanked by two high windows. The dowels of the window screen provide security and sometimes took the place of glass when used with inside shutters. The thick adobe wall sets the scene.

The unique Dutch gable bell tower and plaster strapping surrounding the mission relieve the plain walls and enliven the simple shapes of the building.

The decorative wood gates provide a *chiaroscuro* pattern at the cemetery portal.

The cemetery is adjacent to the church's north wall exit. It has a sweeping view of the valley in a peaceful olive grove glade. The gate uses a simple wood plank cut to provide a pleasing light and dark shadow pattern.

Mission San Miguel Arcángel, 1797

Mission San Miguel Arcángel, 179

Mission San Miguel Arcángel, 1797

The Mission San Miguel Arcángel, is the sixteenth mission founded in California. It was founded on July 25, 1797, by Friar Fermin Lasuén and named for Saint Michael, the chief of the archangels.

Mission San Miguel Arcángel was founded to fill the gap between San Antonio and San Luis Obispo. The mission was built in a valley near where the Salinas and Nacimiento Rivers joined. The Native Americans were so amiable to this mission that a great number attended the first service and fifteen of the children were baptized. Building was started immediately and soon a church was completed and a small village grew around the mission.

A year later a larger church replaced the first; both were mud-roofed and simple in construction. This church was lost in 1806, when a fire destroyed many of the buildings. Included in the loss of the buildings were many of the supplies that the local indigenous population relied on. Fortunately, other nearby missions quickly donated many goods, and within the year the mission was again busy. As a result of the fire, a new large church with tile-roof was planned. For years, the padres had the natives making adobe bricks in preparation of the building. Officially, the new church was started in 1816, but because of the large amount of material prepared in advance, it was completed only two years later.

A friend of Father Martin, artist Estevan Munras from Catalonia, Spain, agreed to decorate the church as a favor. He and some Native Americans he trained decorated the bare walls of the church with intricate designs, which are unusually fine, dramatic graphics: still clear, they have not been retouched or debased.

Originally, Mission San Miguel controlled lands up and down the Salinas River for 50 miles, and operated a rancho at San Simeon, on the coast. In August of 1834, the mission was confiscated as per secularization and the property was dispersed to the Native Americans. The mission itself remained active until 1846. Three days before the United States took over California, Governor Pico sold all the mission lands except the church and priests quarters. William Reed occupied one wing as a personal residence for himself and his family of three. In 1849, a group of outlaws killed Reed, his family, and six servants while robbing him. A posse caught them and took them to Santa Barbara where they were executed.

The mission later became a shop and popular saloon on El Camino Reál. In 1859, some mission properties were restored to the Church, but what was left of San Miguel, was not restored until 1878. The Franciscans returned in 1928 and still use it as a parish church and a monastery. Since that time an amazing recovery has taken place, the years of neglect erased. Today the mission includes the monastery building, with arcade front, the museum, and a beautiful nave where visitors can see the only surviving original Native American and Spanish artwork still visible in the chain of missions.

After the latest earthquake, thanks to a California Mission Foundation grant, the upper nave window was fitted with a steel reinforced frame, which held the wall in place until it could be shored up and reinforced instead of collapsing, while remaining original.

This plain classical façade houses the best frescoed interiors of all the missions. They have been protected and conserved and thankfully not "fully restored." The paint is original; the designs are dramatic and beautifully colored.

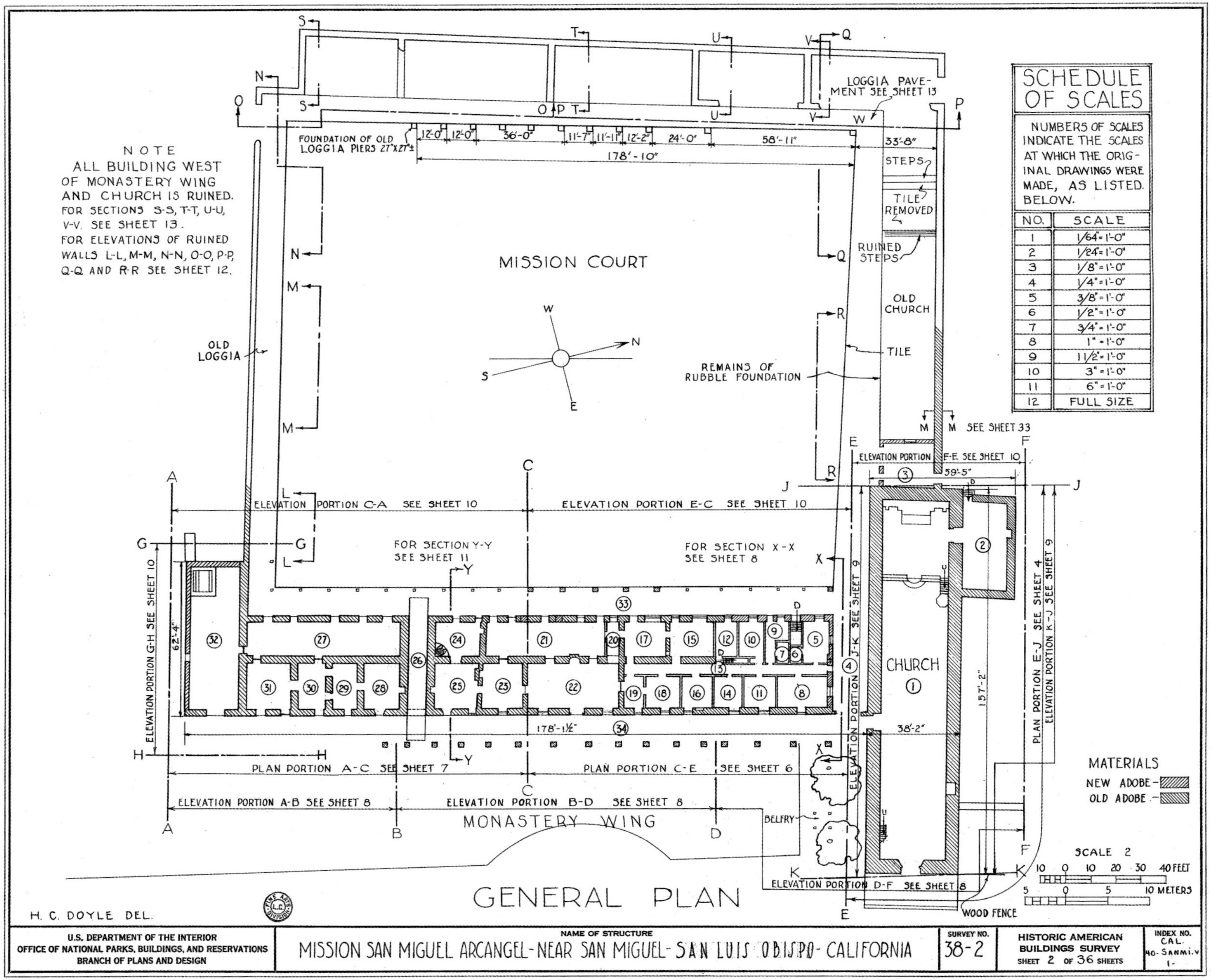

A HABS measured drawing of the plan view of the site, courtyard, and church.

This interior courtyard is the most natural and closest to the original condition of any of the mission courts. Its use of color reflects the ethnic heritage often seen in Mexico and barrios today.

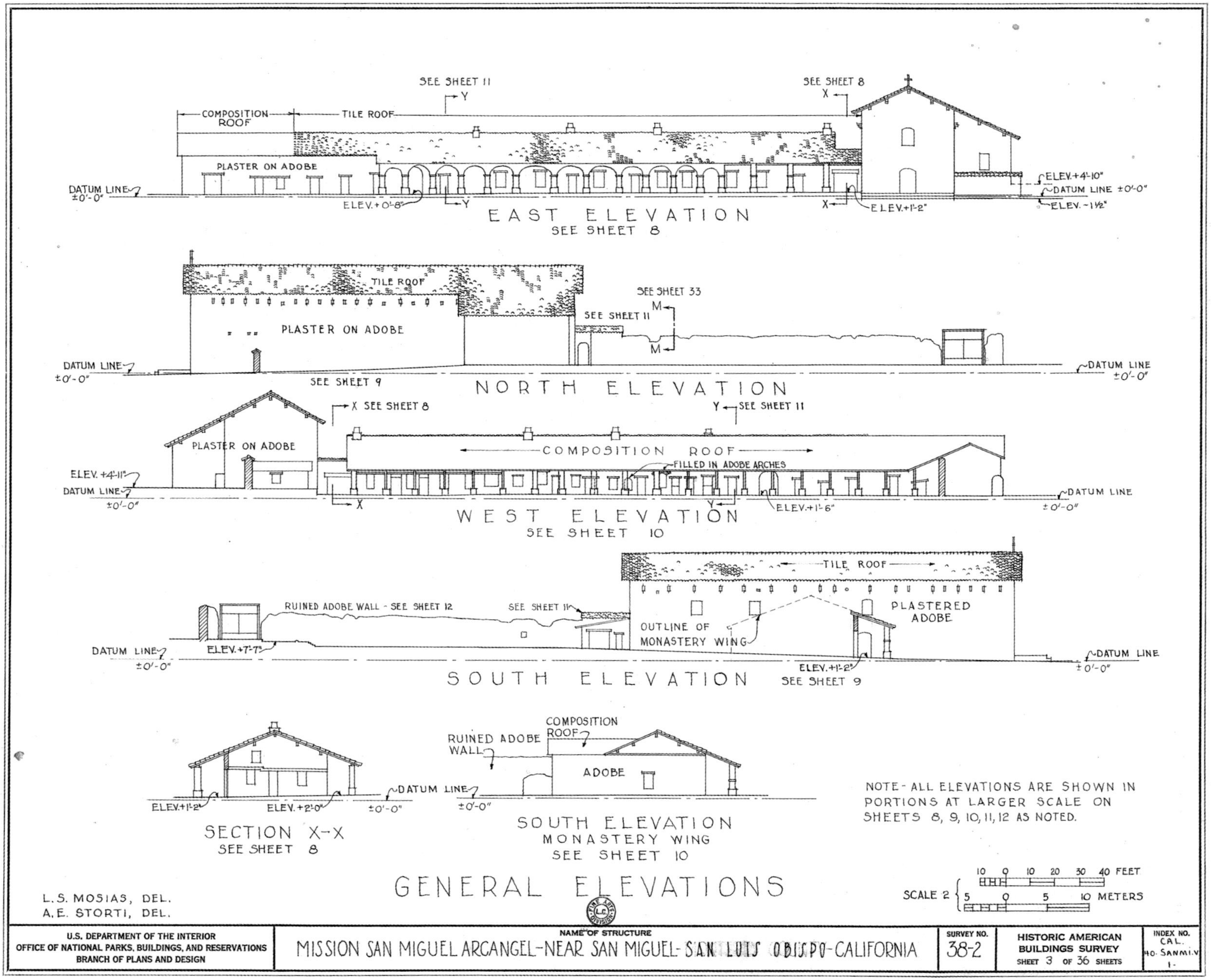

These detailed plans and exterior elevations of the mission, done by the WPA in 1933, are courtesy of the HABS drawing library.

While the restoration of the plaster on the fountains is heavy-handed and looks a little contrived, the shape of the fountain and the onion-shaped, domed pilasters show Moroccan design influence, and provide the mission with a primitive informal charm.

Great architectural effects are found in the light and shadow of the arcades and the fountain details so characteristic of the missions (above and right).

The vertical fins at the end of this arcade herald the side entrance to the sanctuary and provide greater head height as a passageway to the courtyard.

This interior is one of the most picturesque and yet the least restored of all the missions. The altar is topped by an iconic "All-Seeing Eye"; the walls are covered with beautiful and symbolic murals. The sanctuary sports a detached pulpit and colorful canopy under the "Dove of Peace."

This dramatic, beautiful dry-painted *fresco secco* is a giant full-wall shell, the early symbol of baptism and rebirth.

Painted interior details and the delicate colors of these large murals brought life to the flat plaster walls. The Native American parishioners were very intrigued by the graphics and often helped with their own.

This courtyard and perimeter porch capture the feel of rural Mexico, with its casual use of red and blue contrasting colors and aging well-worn detail.

EXIT

The rustic world of mission life shows in the wear and tear of heavy use through the years.

These original corbels show the humble yet distinct design intent and desire for more than just purely utilitarian construction.

This 1930s replica of original work and primitive detail is preserved and still in use in its original state. The yellow portal is original as are the handmade latches and hinge.

Gates, walls, portals, and fences all show the ingenuity and style which accompanied the mission's utilitarian development. Replicas of these original homespun elements are found wherever the better examples of this style are reproduced, being the essence of rustic charm.

This belltower of natural exposed stone is freestanding and very elaborate. It is a *campanario*, or wall belfry, a unique and sturdy example of the early mason's expertise.

Mission San Fernando Rey de España, 1797

Mission San Fernando Rey de España, 1797

Mission San Fernando Rey de España, 1797

The Mission San Fernando Rey de España is the seventeenth mission founded in California. It was founded on September 8, 1797, by Friar Fermin Lasuén and named for King Ferdinand III, king of Castile. He is noted for founding Spain's University of Salamanca in 1243.

The valley had four springs that flowed strong, thus influencing the friar's decision to build there, between the Missions in San Gabriel and San Buenaventura. The first small chapel was raised within two months. Soon a granary, a storeroom, and a weaving room were in operation. A year later, a new church had to be built to accommodate the growing population.

Seven years after its founding, there were more than a thousand converts being housed on the property. In 1806, a third church was dedicated and completed. On December 21, 1812, an earthquake hit that shook the church. It was found to be necessary to install thirty new beams and new buttresses to support the building. These repairs allowed it to survive additional earthquakes over the years.

At its peak in 1819, Mission San Fernando had more than 30,000 grapevines and a winery. In addition to the wine they had a large trade in hides and tallow. There were more than 21,000 head of livestock. The Native Americans became skilled in leatherworking. They made shoes, clothes, and saddles for their own use and for trading. In 1846, Governor Pico made San Fernando his headquarters before abandoning it to the United States Army under the command of Colonel Fremont.

Just before the American occupation, Governor Pico sold most of the buildings to the Pueblo of Los Angeles. Eventually, the buildings fell into disrepair and were damaged by vandalism. After secularization, the roof tiles were removed from the mission for use in other buildings, leaving the adobe walls to melt unprotected.

Secularization at San Fernando Mission started in the 1830s; the California officials began confiscating mission lands, although they usually left the buildings under the control of the Church. From 1834 to 1836, some of the Native Americans stayed but many looked for work in Los Angeles or joined relatives and friends who were still living in the nearby hills.

In 1861, the buildings were returned to the Church, but little was left. The only building that survived was the large adobe building that was alternately called the Mission House, the Long Building, the Monastery, and the Hospice. It was a huge building and many travelers mistook it for the mission itself. In August of 1916, the Landmarks Club turned their attention to Mission San Fernando to begin the restoration. Unfortunately, the restoration looks like new construction and lacks the period charm of some of the other missions.

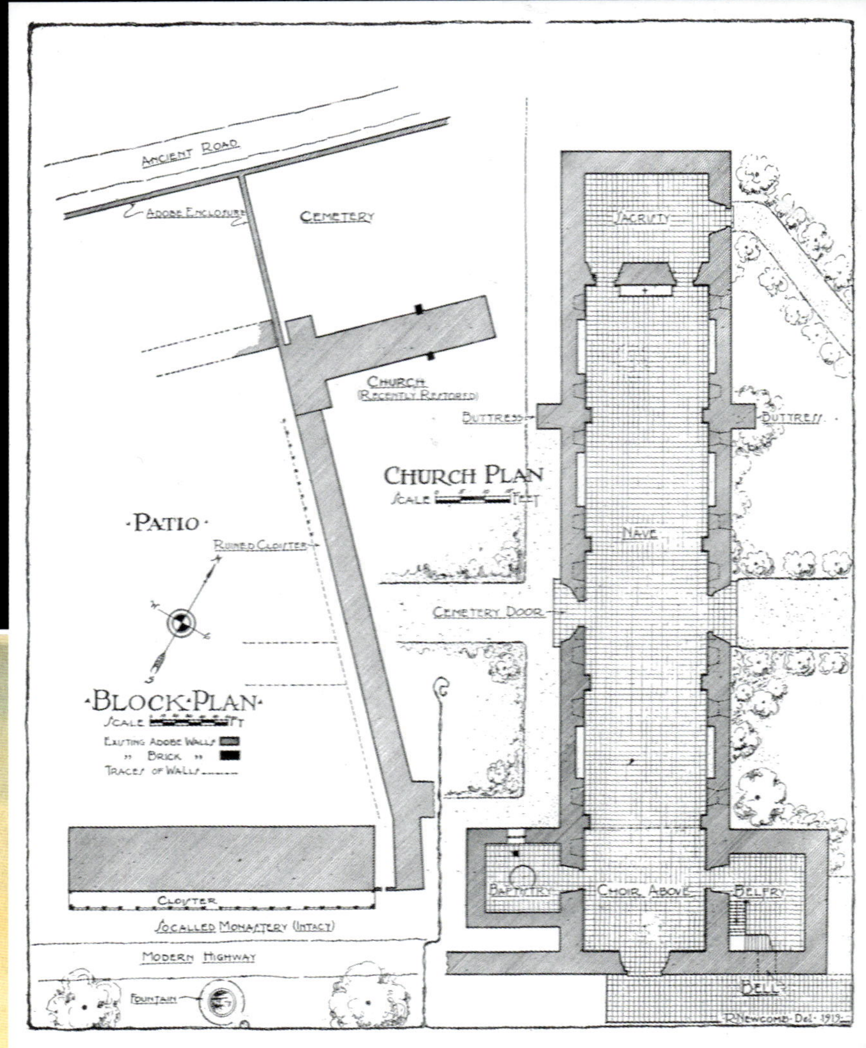

Though a traditional plan, it has fine proportions and creates a grand space.

A Vischer painting of the mission in its early days.

These intriguing graphics stem from the local Native American heritage, enlivening the interior and giving each mission a local flavor (above and opposite).

This dramatic pulpit with hanging overhead carved wood piece and flamboyant *retablo* (opposite) are inspiring and unmatched for their craftsmanship in the rest of the mission chain.

This mission combines both square pilasters and round columns.

One of the most beautiful parts of this mission is the garden setting in front of the convent. A pair of original quatrefoil fountains with the spare native plantings bring out the flavor of Old California.

Mission San Luis Rey de Francia, 1798

Mission San Luis Rey de Francia, 1798

Mission San Luis Rey de Francia, 1798

The Mission San Luis Rey de Francia is the eighteenth mission founded in California. It was founded on June 13, 1798, by Father-President Lasuén and named for King Louis IX, King of France (1215–1270).

Prior to Spanish occupation, the Luiseno people inhabited this area for hundreds of years. Their villages were located in valleys, along streams by the coast and near the mountains. Luiseno homes were dome shaped and constructed of tulles over a branch frame. It was the chief and shaman who saw to it that laws were obeyed in the village.

The establishment of the mission in Alta California was not authorized until the threat of Russian encroachment into the area. In its long history of colonization, Spain had learned that land could be claimed inexpensively by establishing a mission, sending dedicated padres, a handful of soldiers, and a few supplies. With a shortage of Spaniards in the New World, Spain decided to colonize with the indigenous people. The Franciscans were chosen not only to preach to the Native Americans, but to teach them new skills so they could become productive citizens for Spain. Father Antonio Peyri was put in charge of Mission San Luis Rey, from the day of its founding until his departure in January 1832. Between these years the mission became home to approximately 3,000 Native Americans. In their name, and as a result of their labor, the mission cared for more than 50,000 head of livestock. Large sections of the mission's lands were brought under cultivation. Grapes, oranges, olives, wheat, and corn were some of the crops produced. Fields were irrigated by water channeled from the river just north of the mission. The mission was self-sustaining: its buildings were constructed of local materials, such as adobe, fired clay bricks, and wooden timbers. By 1830, the mission was the largest building in California.

After Mexico won its independence from Spain in 1821, the law of secularization was passed. The law stated that the land was to be handed over to the Native Americans. However, Mission San Luis Rey came under the control of various secular administrators, several of whom managed to gain the titles to large portions of former mission land and thousands of cattle and sheep, leaving nothing to the Luisenos.

From 1847–1857 the mission was used as an operational base by U.S. soldiers. However, after the military vacated the mission, it lay abandoned until 1892.

Certainly one of the most beautiful and beautifully preserved missions is San Luis Rey, named after the King of France. At right, an Edward Borein etching from the early 1900s shows the mission in operation, and below how it stands today. The Moroccan influence of the plaster strapping, domes, and towers, along with its sheer size and lively massing, create an impressive presence.

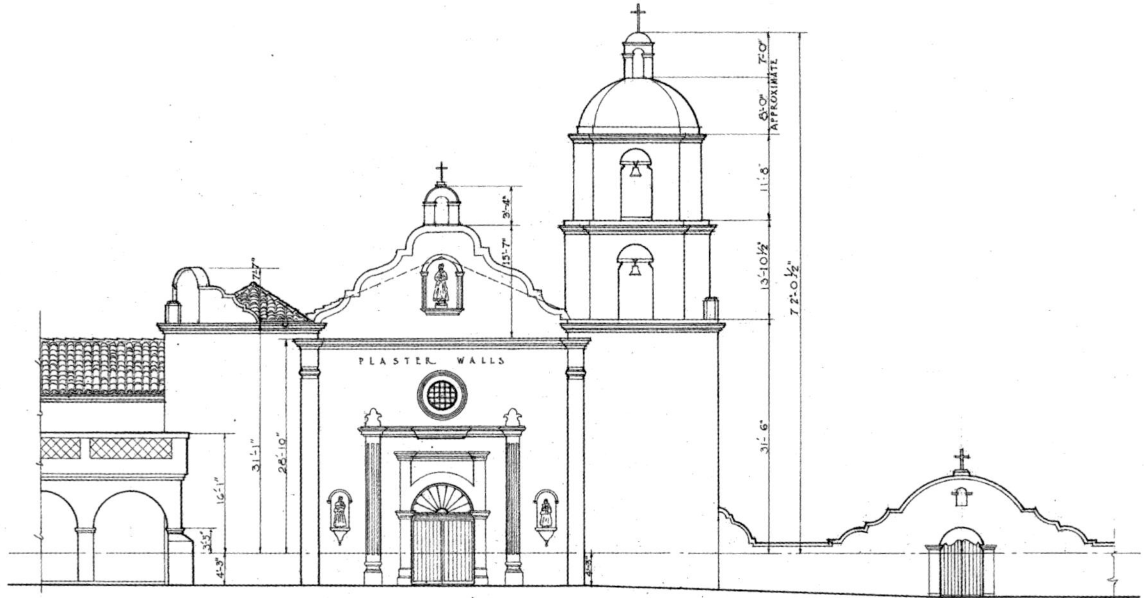

FRONT ELEVATION (SOUTH)
SCALE 3/32" = 1'-0

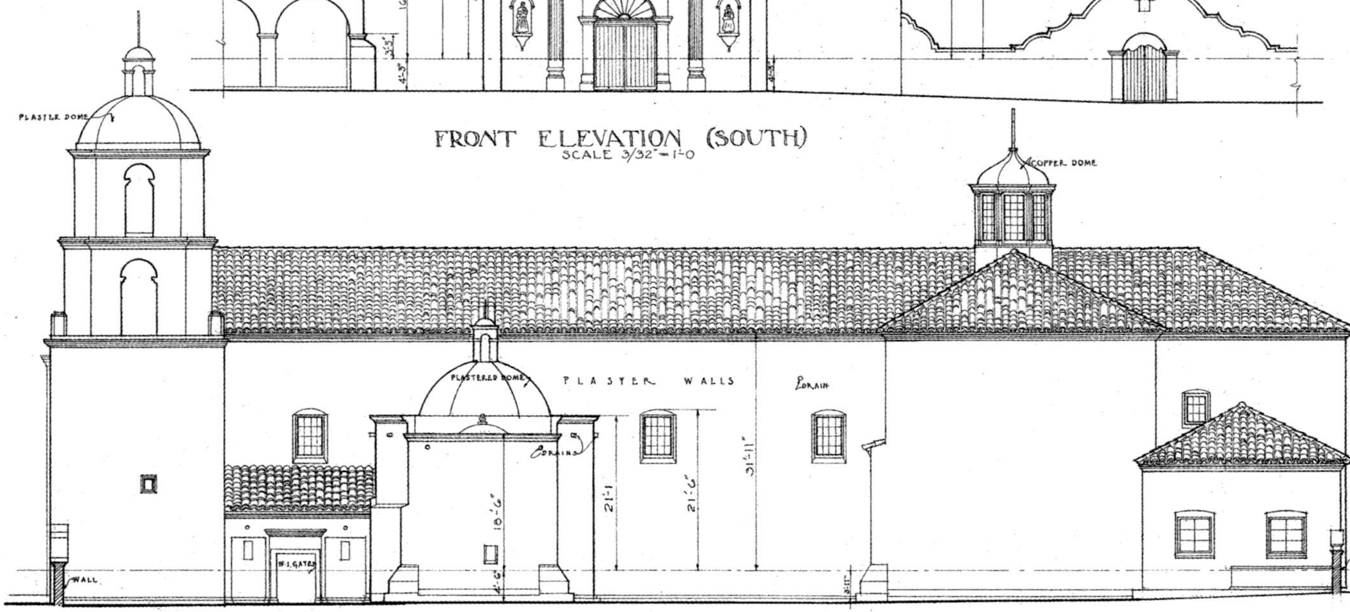

EAST ELEVATION
SCALE 3/32" = 1'-0

0 4 8 12 16 18 24 28 FEET

0 1 2 3 4 5 6 7 8 9 10 11 12 METERS

WILLIAM H PAULUS DEL

WORKS PROGRESS ADMINISTRATION OFFICIAL PROJECT NO 265-6907 UNDER DIRECTION OF UNITED STATES DEPARTMENT OF THE INTERIOR NATIONAL PARK SERVICE, BRANCH OF PLANS AND DESIGN	NAME OF STRUCTURE MISSION - SAN LUIS REY DE FRANCIA OCEANSIDE - SAN DIEGO COUNTY - CALIFORNIA	SURVEY NO. CAL 42	HISTORIC AMERICAN BUILDINGS SURVEY SHEET 6 OF 25 SHEETS	LIBRARY OF CONGRESS INDEX NUMBER

The original church is believed to have had twin towers.

The tiered bell tower with chamfered corners is very similar to the Santa Barbara Mission.

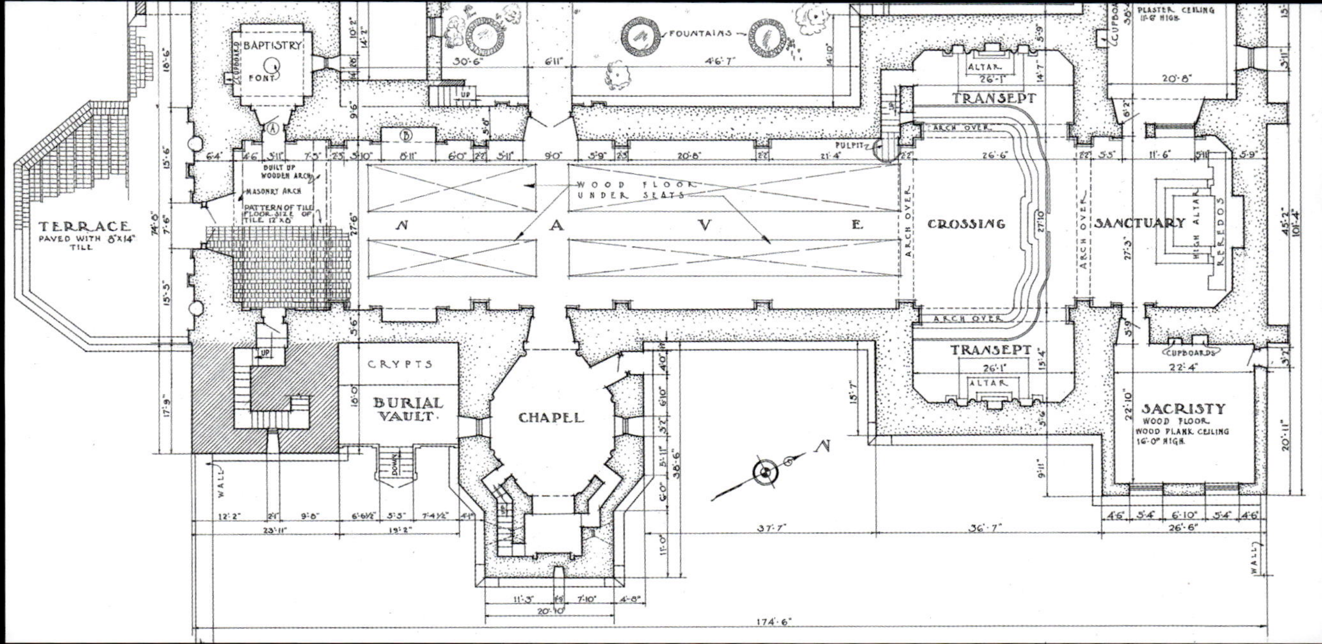

The model and measured drawing show the size of this mission. Its impressive size and two-story courtyard with attached cemetery makes it the largest mission and the most integrated composition. These larger missions were built by accretion. New buildings and courtyards were added as the church grew over time.

This mission has the most impressive interior of any. The crossing has a beautiful octagonal wood-faced dome with lantern. The restored painting and trim is colorful and tasteful. The checkerboard patterns and wild pastel colors give the interior a great flair, along with its wall-hung pulpit. The separate baptistery and funeral chapels adjacent to the main sanctuary add great solemnity to the space.

The choir loft over the entry is grand under a deep arch and south-facing round solstice window. It bears a striking resemblance to that of Santa Barbara's choir and single round window, but probably predates it.

The doorways are modeled after the fifteenth-century churches in Spain. The portals' scalloped shadow pattern, reminiscent of a shell, and decorative paint make the plain walls come alive. This cross axis bisects the church from its side cemetery chapel across to the

Original baptistery behind newer wrought iron grillwork gates.

This funeral chapel's side door leads directly into the cemetery. Under the dome, the natural light comes in at the high right (morning light) side of the altar, highlighting the statue. The symmetry creates a solemn and serene space.

The sanctuary contains a wide variety of window sizes and shapes, which gives the main church nave a great deal of architectural interest

Fanciful decorations make this the most colorful interior of all the missions, with some of the finest trim.

The baptismal font is found in a small side chapel at the entry to the church.

Stencil decoration, originally done with cut out leather patterns, is used around the church perimeter and

The quality of the work and the refined use of color show the intensity of the effort to make the church important and inviting to the congregation.

The architectural detail on this 1825 lantern has hints of neoclassical roots. The plaster strapping frames the elevation.

The fluid shape and stark white walls give this mission its great Spanish cathedral feel. The baptistery dome echoes the Cathedral at Cadiz, a port in Spain. The exacting plaster trim shows the care and prosperous flamboyance with which this church was built.

Sunlight plays on the portal looking out from inside the cemetery.

The flamboyant shape of the entry gate profile creates a special sense of place for the cemetery.

The convent arcade surrounds a protected courtyard.

Solid massing and a classic covered arcade, along with fine detail, create the setting.

Architectural details give the church its character.

This original circular adobe outbuilding, above, and the simple multiple fountains show the use of masonry construction and inherent strength of the original mission.

Mission Santa Inés Virgen y Mártir, 1804

Mission Santa Inés Virgen y Mártir, 1804

Mission Santa Inés Virgen y Mártir, 1804

Mission Santa Inés Virgen y Mártir, (sometimes spelled Santa Ynez) was founded on September 17, 1804, by Father Estévan Tapís, who succeeded Father Fermin Lasuén as President of the California mission chain.

The mission site was chosen as a midway point between Mission Santa Barbara and Mission La Purísima Concepción, and was designed to relieve overcrowding at those two missions, and to serve the Native Americans living east of the Coast Range.

Most of the original church was destroyed on December 21, 1812, in an earthquake centered near Santa Barbara that damaged or destroyed most of the California missions. The quake also severely damaged other mission buildings on site, but the complex was not abandoned. A new church, constructed with 5-foot-thick walls and great pine beams brought from nearby Figueroa Mountain, was dedicated on July 4, 1817.

Unfortunately, on February 21, 1824, a soldier beat a young Chumash Indian and sparked a revolt. When the fighting was over, many of the Native Americans left to join other tribes in the mountains—only a few remained at the mission. In 1833, the missions in California were secularized, and their land given in land grants to settlers.

In 1843, California's Mexican governor granted 34,499 acres of Santa Ynez Valley land to the first Bishop of California, who established the first seminary in California. The college was closed in 1881, since by then the mission was disintegrating. A family lived on the mission grounds in the 1890s and did some repairs, but much of the complex collapsed in 1894. Reconstruction of the mission was undertaken, though major restoration was not possible until 1947, when the Hearst Foundation donated money to this and many other missions to pay for the repairs. The restoration continues to this day, and the Capuchin Franciscan Fathers conserve the mission.

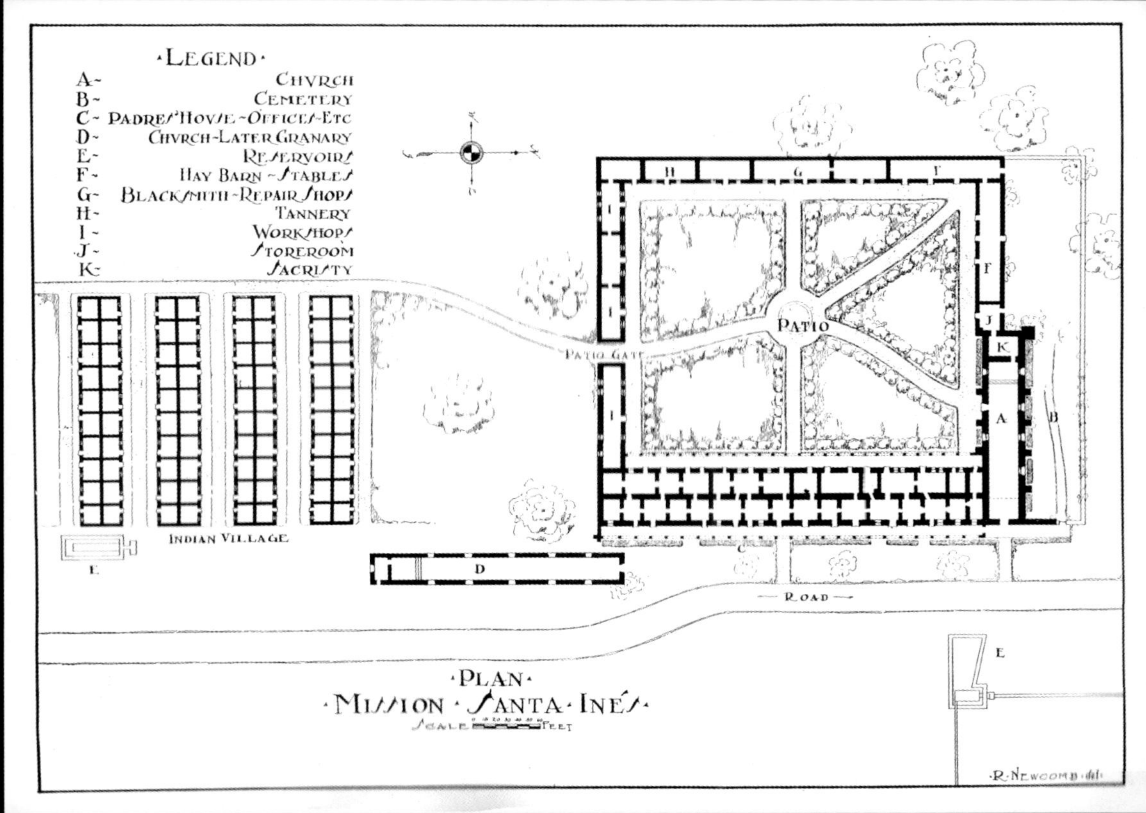

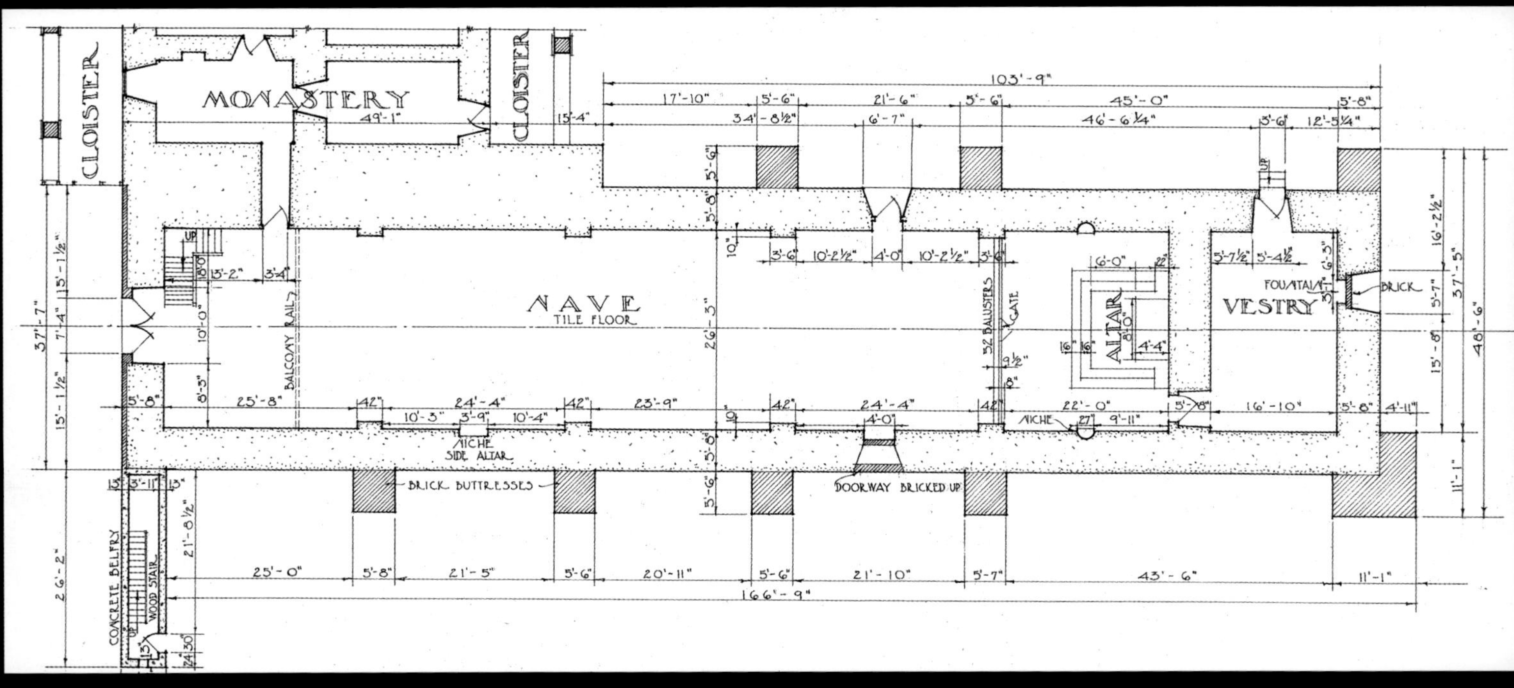

The HABS as-built site plan and floor plan show the mission as it has stood since 1804.

The vacant field remains today, giving a broadside view of the mission. The view shows the buttresses alternating with window placement, giving this composition its steady, solid, and balanced strength.

A Santa Ynez valley view from the mission.

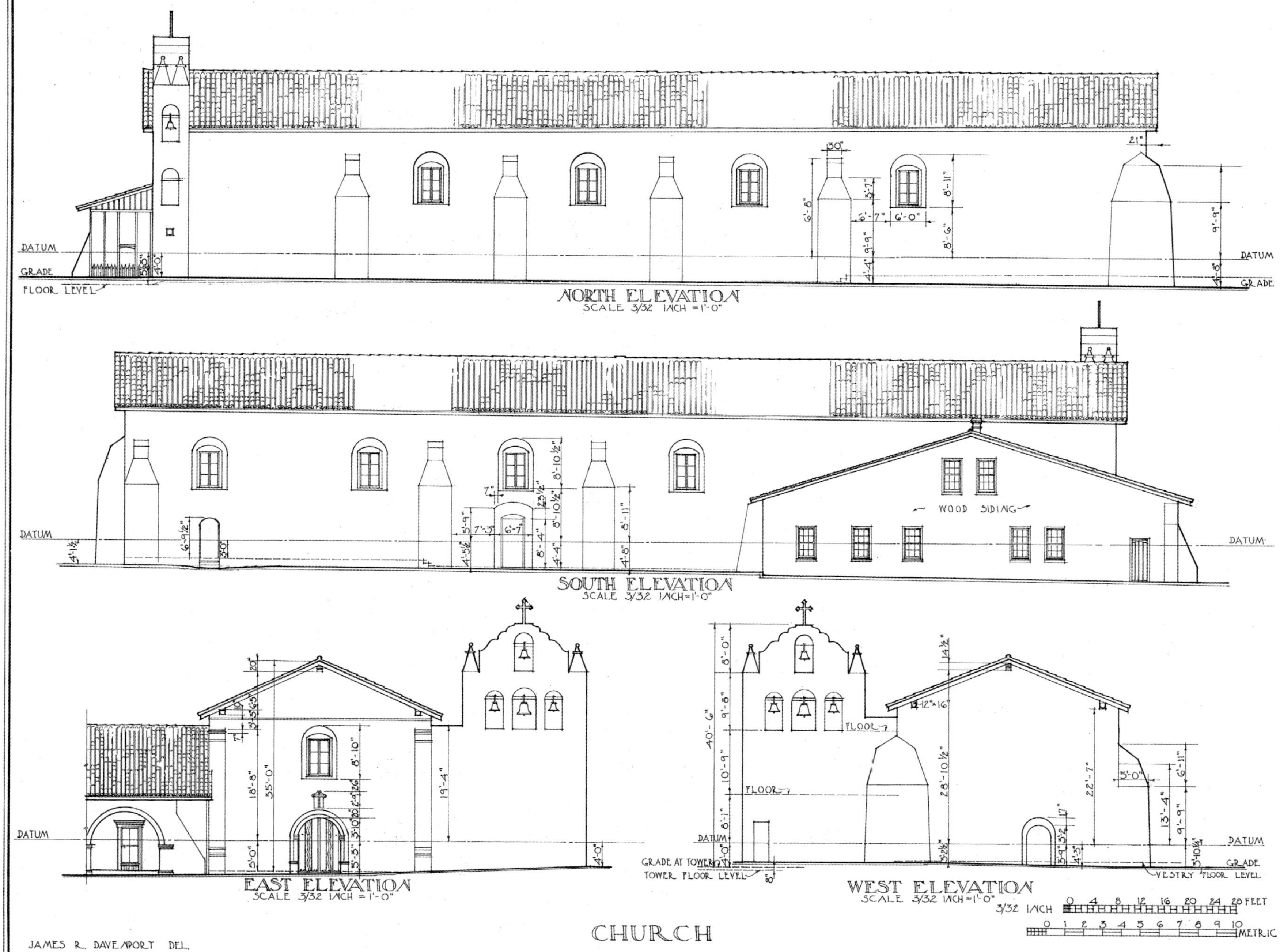

WORKS PROGRESS ADMINISTRATION
OFFICIAL PROJECT NO 265-6907.
UNDER DIRECTION OF UNITED STATES DEPARTMENT OF THE INTERIOR
NATIONAL PARK SERVICE, BRANCH OF PLANS AND DESIGN

NAME OF STRUCTURE

SANTA YNEZ MISSION

SOLVANG – SANTA BARBARA COUNTY – CALIFORNIA

SURVEY NO. CAL 24

HISTORIC AMERICAN BUILDINGS SURVEY
SHEET 2 OF 11 SHEETS

· TOUR · BEGINS HERE ·
PLEASE DO NOT LEAN ON MODEL

The free-spirited pinnacles, round forms, and pierced bell towers, or *campanarios*, are evidence of the Native influence on the early Spanish parish architecture.

Backside of the bell tower.

Sunny arcades like this one are characteristic of the style.

OLD MISSION
GIFT SHOP

The choir loft shows the effects of the Victorian-era makeover.

This wall painting shows a Victorian influence, and is surely more intricate than the original wall decoration.

Detail of the intricate brickwork railing over the arcade.

The balcony brick balustrade adds an elegant detail to the mission balcony.

Mission San Rafael Arcángel, 1817

Mission San Rafael Arcángel, 1817

Mission San Rafael Arcángel, 1817

The mission originally was established to serve as a convalescent hospital to the many sick neophytes (Christianized Native Americans) from Mission San Francisco. It was named after Saint Rafael, the angel of healing. The pleasant climate of the north shore of the San Francisco Bay was rumored to restore health to the sick Native Americans and soon parishioners from Mission San Francisco, as well as other missions, began sending their sick to this healthy locale.

San Rafael was never intended to be a full-fledged mission, but with significant growth due to the success of its rehabilitation programs, it was founded as a full mission on October 18, 1822. By 1828, there were more than 1,000 Native Americans living and working at the Mission San Rafael Arcángel.

The Native Americans who moved to the mission were taught trades in order to become productive members of the community. The padres helped them to become expert cattlemen, boat makers, blacksmiths, carpenters, and weavers. Although it started as a hospital mission, it soon became fully self-supporting. Gaining more economic stability than the Mission San Francisco, the Mission San Rafael boasted the most animals of any California mission.

In 1822, when the mission chapel was built, no surrounding quadrangle was constructed. San Rafael remains one of the few missions in the Alta California chain without a centering quadrangle. The mission suffered many military encounters during its short 17 years, but it remained extremely productive.

The original church was demolished and this smaller church rebuilt as a memorial structure.

The re-built interior, while beautiful, has a more contemporary feel than the surviving original missions.

MISSION
GIFT SHOP

Mission San Francisco Solano, 1823

Mission San Francisco Solano, 1823

Mission San Francisco Solano, 1823

Father José Altimira founded the Mission San Francisco Solano on July 4, 1823. It was the twenty-first of California's twenty-one missions and was the last mission established in the Alta California Chain.

Not only was Mission San Francisco Solano the final mission established in the Alta California Chain, it was also the northernmost. Father José Altimira, known for his unruliness, desired to move away from his post at Mission Delores. Without permission from the church, he traveled northward where he established the Mission San Francisco Solano.

This mission was the only mission not condoned by the church. It also was the only mission established after Mexico won its independence. Rather than proposing his new mission to the church, Father Altimira asked the governor directly for permission. He wanted to combine Missions San Francisco de Asís, San Rafael Arcángel, and San Francisco Solano into one mission, in this newly chosen location. The governor gave his permission, but the church would only sanction this mission if Father Altimira left the other missions alone. With this compromise, Father Altimira began construction on his new mission in 1823.

While the Solano mission did not receive much help from the other missions, it did receive a lot of support from the nearby Russian outpost, Fort Ross. Many Native Americans flocked to the mission in search of a warmer climate and an easier lifestyle. What they found instead was an oppressive leader. The Native Americans grew tired of being oppressed by Father Altimira and in 1828 attacked the father and set fire to the mission. After Father Altimira fled back to Spain, the mission stabilized. Although it had a rough economic beginning, the mission achieved success after Father Altimira. By 1830, almost 1,000 Native Americans lived and worked at the mission.

General Vallejo, the comandante of the San Francisco presidio who owned great estates in the North Bay area, became the first administrator after secularization. All of the mission livestock was moved to his ranches, along with everything else he could take. Even the vines and pear trees were dug up and replanted on his property. He gathered the Native Americans to work on his own ranches, and let them work for their room and board.

The chapel built at San Francisco Solano still stands today. It is 105 feet long and 22 feet wide. Made of thick adobe walls, the chapel had a tile roof and was surrounded by twenty-seven other rooms.

The character of the building is much more rustic and frontier styled than the missions farther south.

The space gains its charm primarily from its fine proportions, many windows, lively color, and simple understated elegance.

Small pane windows provide light on both sides of the sanctuary. The deep wall area gives the building mass without sacrificing the interior light.

The variety and use of the window shapes has an abstract minimalist look which appeals to our modern taste.

Windows are made of hand-adzed wood with small panes slotted into fine trim, and chamfered corners showing the craftsmanship and care taken to make the mission a sturdy and handsome structure.

The restoration was done using original techniques. Stripped log beams and thatch were used for the roof structure and leather strapping in place of nails.

Rustic details and common materials used in unusual ways make the structure a delightful surprise, while the heavy walls and weathered patina give it a gravitas worthy of respect.

The feeling of the western frontier is brought forth here with unfinished wood, adobe walls, and simple direct details. The soldiers quarters next door is so true to form it could be used as a frontier movie set.

Old California Adobes

Adobe Structures Built During the Early Mission Period

El Molino Viejo, San Marino, 1816

El Molino Viejo, San Marino, 1816

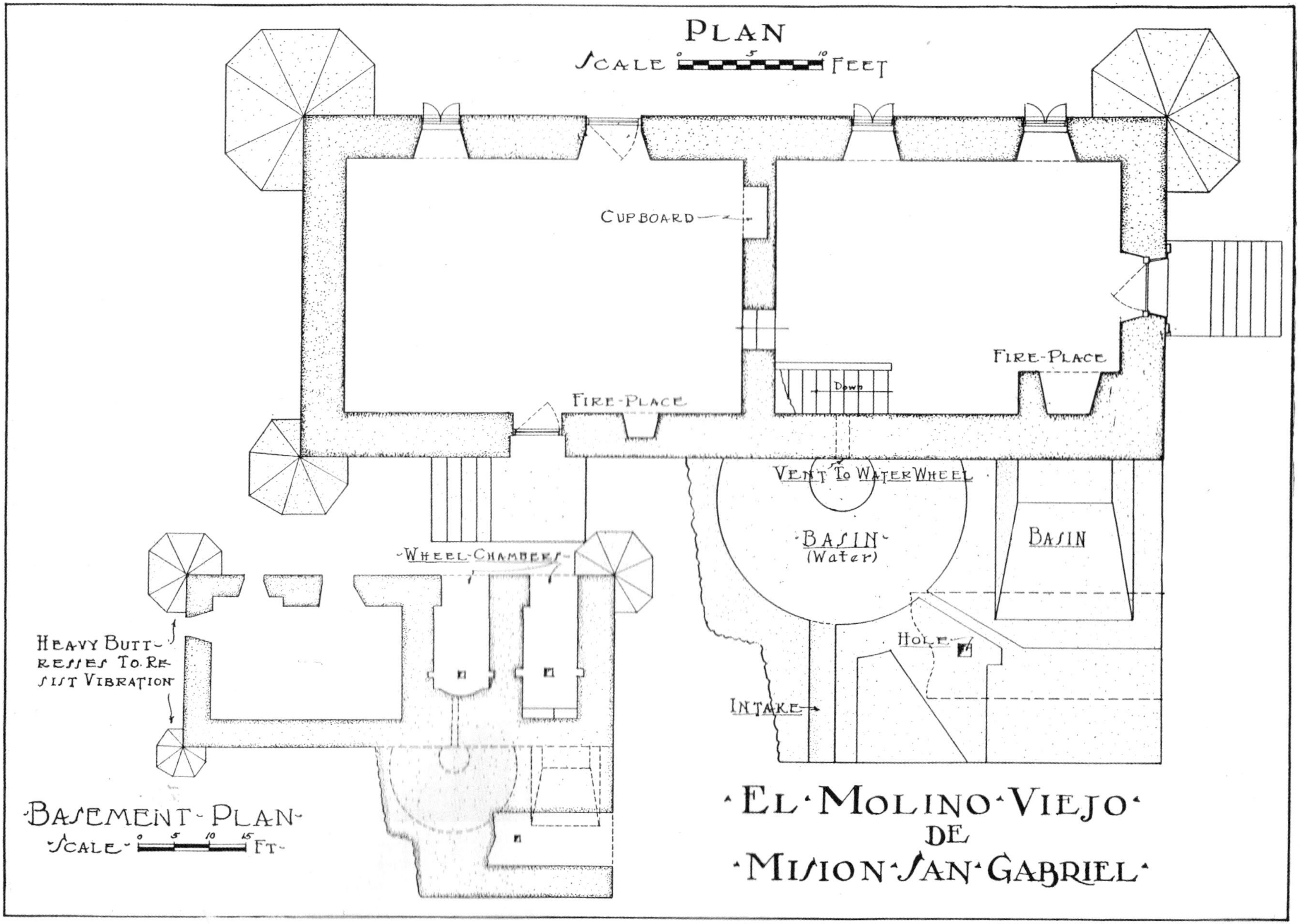

El Molino Viejo, also known as The Old Mill, is a former grist mill in the San Rafael Hills of present day San Marino, California. It was built in 1816 by Father José Maria de Zalvidea from the Mission San Gabriel Arcángel (San Gabriel Mission). It is the oldest commercial building in Southern California, and was one of the first ten sites in Los Angeles County to be listed on the National Register of Historic Places.

PRESENTED BY
THE DAN MURPHY FOUNDATION
TO
THE CALIFORNIA HISTORICAL SOCIETY
MODEL BY-

Exterior details

Interior character

El Presidio, Santa Barbara, 1782

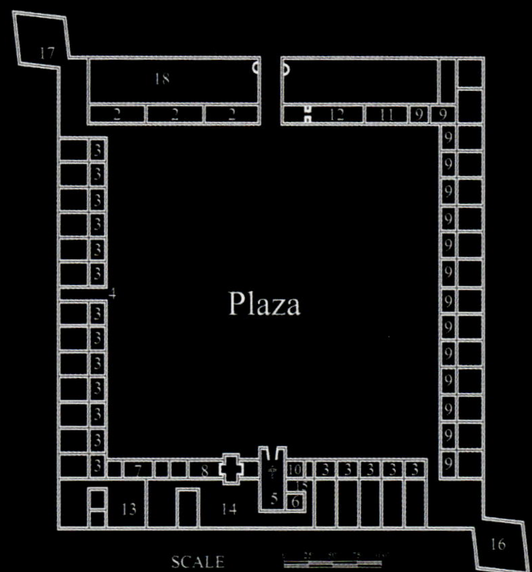

Plan of Santa Barbara Presidio 1788

1 - MAIN ENTRANCE
2 - STOREHOUSES
3 - FAMILY HOUSES
4 - FALSE GATE
5 - CHURCH
6 - SACRISTY
7 - ALFEREZ' SUITE
8 - SCOMMANDANT'S SUITE
9 - FAMILY HOUSES
10 - CHAPLAN'S SUITE
11 - SERGENT'S HOUSE
12 - GUARD ROOM and QUARTERS
13 - ALFEREZ' CORRALS, KITCHEN
14 - COMMANDANT CORRALS, KITCHEN
15 - CHAPLAIN'S CORRAL
16 - WESTERN BASTION
17 - EASTER BASTION
18 - CORRALS

This is the plan of the Presidio sent by the Commandant Goycoechea to Governor Fages in 1788

El Presidio Reál de Santa Barbara, 1782

El Presidio Reál de Santa Barbara, also known as the Royal Presidio of Santa Barbara, was a military installation in Santa Barbara, California. It was built by Spain in 1782, with the mission of defending the Second Military District in California. The site of the Presidio was chosen by Felipe de Neve, the first governor of Las Californias. Perceiving that the coast at Santa Barbara was vulnerable to attack, he located a spot near a harbor which was sheltered from severe storms. In addition, there was an ample supply of both building materials and water nearby. Construction began on April 21, 1782, and Padre Junípero Serra blessed the site. By the next year, a temporary facility had been completed, and a wheat field planted by the local Chumash Indians of Chief Yanonalit. The early Presidio consisted of mud and brush walls around a quadrangle 330 feet on a side. The post had 61 officers and men in 1783. The Presidio was built as a fortress, and therefore included a strong outer wall with an open parade ground on all sides affording clear visibility. While it was never attacked by a strong military force during its sixty years of operation, the Presidio was subject to the assaults of nature. Several devastating earthquakes in the early nineteenth century destroyed much of the structure which has been rebuilt today to exacting standards that studiously replicate the original

Casa de la Guerra, Santa Barbara, 1828

This house was the residence of the fifth commandant of the Presidio de Santa Barbara, José de la Guerra y Noriega, from 1828 until his death in 1858. Descendants of de la Guerra lived in the home until 1943. The site is currently owned and operated by the Santa Barbara Trust for Historic Preservation as a historic house museum.

This model shows the extent and original layout of the de la Guerra house.

CASA De La GUERRA

THE PRESIDIO AND PUEBLO OF MONTERREY UPPER CALIFORNIA

El Presidio Reál de San Carlos de Monterey, Monterey, 1768

Visitador General José de Gálvez, the viceroyalty of New Spain, received the following orders: "Occupy and fortify San Diego and Monterey for God and the King of Spain." Two years later, a small expedition led by captain Gaspar de Portolá and Father Junípero Serra officially took possession for the upper Las Californias Province, what is now central California, via the establishment of El Presidio Reál de San Carlos de Monterey (the Royal Garrison of Saint Charles of Monterey).

This chapel's recent restoration has used Victorian details, like ceiling corbels, that leave the interior a little out of sync with the original structure. On the positive side, original wall mural remnants were found and preserved in place under glass.

Old Customhouse, Monterey, 1827

The Old Customhouse is a Spanish Colonial style adobe structure built around 1827 by the Mexican government in the Pueblo Monterey California. The Customhouse is the state's first designated California Historical Landmark. In 1821, Mexico won independence fron Spain in the Mexican War of Independence, and for nearly 25 years Monterey was in the Mexican Pueblo of Monterey. Under Mexicar rule the trade restrictions were lifted and coastal ports were opened to foreign trade. This drew in trade from British, American, anc South American traders.

To collect customs duties (tax monies) at the Monterey Bay port, the Mexican government built the Customhouse, making it the oldes government building in present day California. On July 7, 1846, during the Mexican-American War, Commodore John Drake Sloa raised the American Flag at the Customhouse, declaring California part of the United States.

An early photo of the Customhouse shows how well it has been preserved through today.

The presidio buildings are gone and only a rolling open hillside remains. The model shows its configuration.

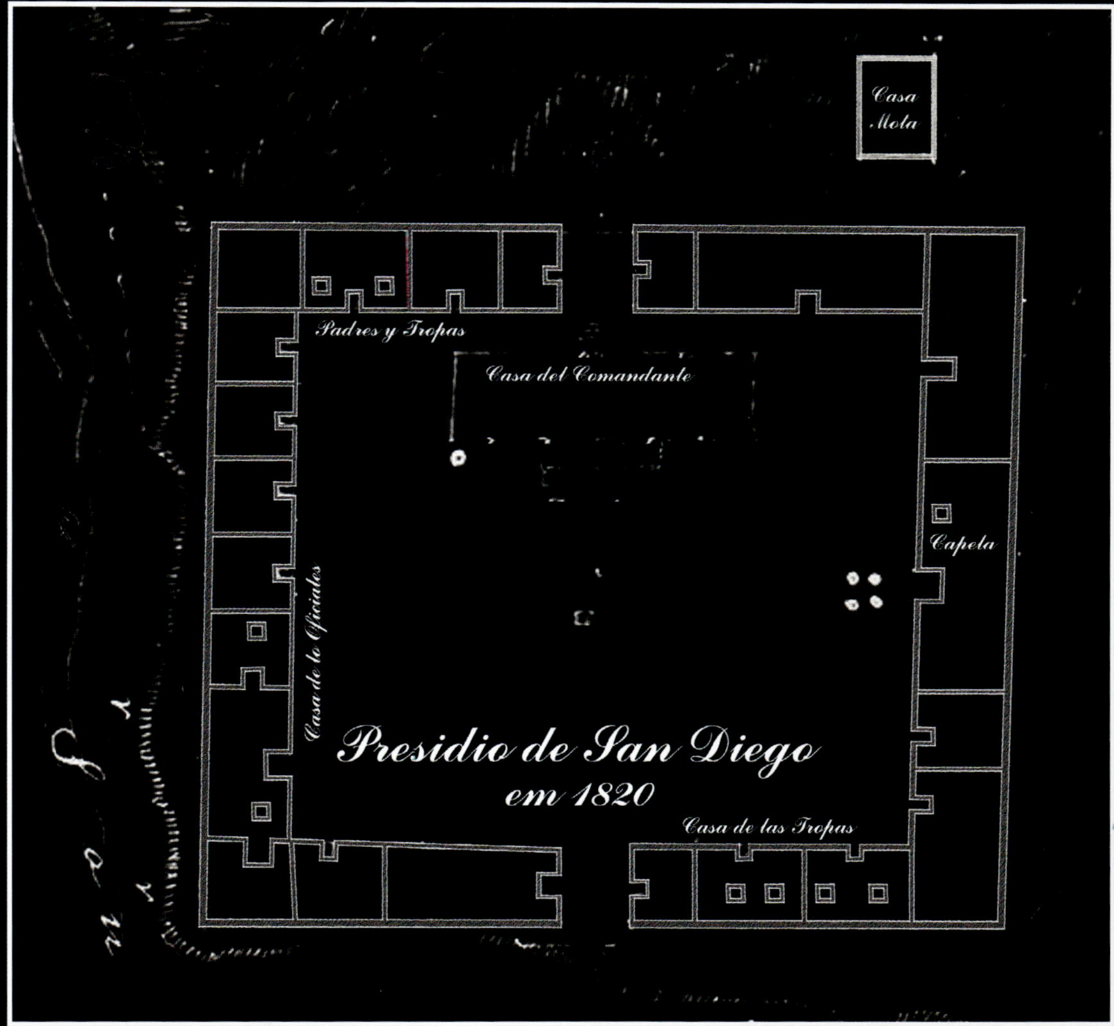

El Presidio Reál de San Diego, 1769

El Presidio Reál de San Diego (Royal Garrison of San Diego) is a historical fort established on May 14, 1769, by Commandant Pedro Fages for Spain. It was the first permanent European settlement on the Pacific Coast. As the first of the presidios and Spanish missions in California, it was the base of operations for the Spanish colonization of California. The Mission San Diego de Alcalá later moved a few miles away.

Presidio of San Diego

Mission Architectural Elements

San Diego

Carmel

Bell Towers: *Campanarios*

A bell tower is a tower which is designed to hold bells, even if it has none. In the European tradition, such a tower most commonly serves as part of a church and contains church bells. In missions the pierced-wall bell tower originated in Moorish Mudejar Spain but was developed in North America, first found in the Yucatan area and New Mexico and then introduced throughout the Alta California chain. The best examples are found at the San Gabriel and San Diego Missions.

San Juan Capistrano

Santa Inés

San Gabriel

a Purísima

Carmel

San Luis Rey

San Juan Capistrano

San Juan Bautista

Carmel

Jose

Santa Barbara Presidio

dad

San Francisco

Juan Capistrano

Ventura

Santa Barbara

San Migu

Solano

Carmel

Santa Barbara Presidio

La Purísima

Santa Inés

San Luis Obispo

San Fernando

San Juan Capistrano

San Diego

Soledad

San Juan Bautista

San Francisco

San Miguel

San Jose

Santa Barbara

Santa Clara

San Luis Rey

San Gabriel

San Antonio

Buenaventura

Naves

In Romanesque and Gothic Christian abbeys, cathedral basilica, and church architecture, the nave is the central approach to the high altar, the main body of the church. "Nave" (Medieval Latin *navis*, "ship") was probably suggested for the keel shape of its vaulting. This central approach with processional requirements defined the exterior, central-entry architectural solution seen in most of the missions.

San Juan Capistrano

Buenaventura

San Luis Obispo

Santa Barbara

San Fernando

Santa Inés

San Francisco

San Jose

San Luis Rey

San Miguel

Santa Clara

San Juan Bautista

San Rafael

San Diego

Soledad

San Fernando

Solano

San Antonio

Solano

La Purísima, padre chapel

La Purísima, main church

Carmel

Santa Barbara Presidio

San Gabriel

San Fernando

Choir Lofts

In missions the choir is usually a loft space over the entry. It houses the organ and can accommodate the singing choir or accompanying instruments. The stair can be inside the belltower like Carmel or outside the building, as it is at San Diego.

Buenaventura

Solano

Solano

La Purísima, chapel

Santa Barbara

Santa Inés

San Luis Rey

San Juan Capistrano

Carmel

La Purísima

San Juan Bautista

Santa Barbara

San Jose

San Luis Rey

La Purísima

Carmel

San Diego

San Juan Capistrano

Solano

San Antonio

Carmel

San Miguel

San Luis Rey

Doors

San Miguel

Solano

San Jose

San Juan Bautista

Santa Barbara

San Jose

Santa Barbara

San Fernando

Carmel

San Juan Capistrano

Santa Inés

The Missions in Historic Art

Here is a sampling of artists who recorded most or all of the missions in a series of works by their own hand.

Carmel

San Francisco

Santa Barbara

San Buenaventura

In 1875, he settled in Santa Barbara, California, where he would live out his days. Ford travelled by horse and buggy to each of the twenty-one Spanish missions in California, where he created a historically important portfolio of watercolors, oils, and etchings. His depictions of the missions were (in part) responsible for the revival of interest in the state's Spanish heritage, and indirectly for the restoration of the missions themselves. In 1883, Ford published his *Etchings of the Franciscan Missions of California*, and exhibited his works at the 1893 Chicago World's Fair. The hallmarks of Ford's images are exquisite brushwork and tonal mastery in all mediums, which make his works highly prized. Ford died in 1894 in Santa Barbara.

Santa Barbara

San Gabriel

San Luis Obispo

San Francisco

Edwin Deakin (1838–1923)

An aristocrat from England with minimal artistic training, Edwin Deakin settled in Northern California where he painted landscapes of ruins, historic architecture, and scenes—romantic views of castles and quaint English villages. Deakin was born in Sheffield, England, and came to America in 1856, living first in Chicago, where he earned some reputation for portraits of Civil War heroes. In 1870, he moved to San Francisco and set up a studio and soon was very much a part of the local art scene.

From 1887 to 1890, Deakin painted in Europe and exhibited at the Paris Salon. From then until his death in 1923, he lived in Berkeley on a large tract of land he purchased where he built a mission-style studio. Although Deakin would expand his repertory to include architectural subjects like the California missions and still life paintings, he never abandoned landscapes.

Carmel

Santa Barbara

Solano

Santa Cruz

San Francisco

Santa Cruz

San Luis Rey

Carmel

Carleton E. Watkins was born in Oneonta, Oswego County, New York, on November 11, 1829. He was the youngest of five children of a Scottish innkeeper. During his youth, he became acquainted with Collis P. Huntington, who frequented his father's hotel. Soon after the discovery of gold, both young men went to California. *The Franciscan Missions of California* album contains 35 albumen prints taken by Carleton E. Watkins, circa 1876–1882. Watkins probably began photographing the missions while returning from a trip to Southern California in 1876, along the newly constructed Southern Pacific Railroad line. The album is believed to be the earliest general photographic collection produced of the California missions, and includes photographs of most of the missions found in the state.

San Jose

San Luis Rey

San Antonio

San Diego

Glossary

ADOBE: Sun-dried bricks made of clay mixed with straw and sometimes horse manure, then baked in the sun. Also refers to structures made of this material.

ALTA: Spanish for "upper." Used in Alta California, the Spanish territory that included present day California.

ALTAR: A raised platform where offerings or sacrifices are made: the Communion table.

ALTA CALIFORNIA: The Spanish territory, including present day California.

APSE: A domed or vaulted semicircular recess, found most frequently at the east end of a church.

ARROYO: A brook, rivulet, or small stream.

ARCADE: A roofed walkway, one side composed of a series of arches. An arcade provided a cool place to walk in summertime, was dry in winter, and helped protect adobe walls from direct rainfall.

ASISTENCIA: In California, an outlying mission station which had a chapel but no residents. A subordinate satellite outpost mission.

BEE-HIVE OVEN: A wood-fired, cone-shaped brick oven, used for baking bread.

BELL TOWER: A tall vertical structure which contains bells; a bell tower is a variety of *campanario*.

BUTTRESS: A stone or brick structure to support or brace a heavy wall.

CAMPANARIO: A wall with openings for bells (Sp. *campanas*).

CAMPO SANTO: Cemetery, literally "Holy Field," the place where baptized Catholics, including Native American neophytes, were buried.

CENOTAPH: A monument built to honor people whose remains are buried elsewhere.

CHANCEL: The area in a church containing the altar and seats for the clergy.

CUPOLA: A small rounded structure built on top of a roof or bell tower.

CONVENTO: Wing of a mission building or the set of rooms in which the missionaries lived.

ESPANADA: Separate pierced bell-wall such as that found at Mission San Diego or Mission San Gabriel.

EL CAMINO REÁL: The Royal Highway, which began near the tip of Baja California and connected the settlements of Baja and Alta California.

ESTANCIA: An outlying mission ranch for the pasturing of livestock (horses, cattle, sheep, goats, or pigs) or for the cultivation of crops such as wheat, corn, beans, or grapes.

EYE OF GOD: The wide open eye symbolizes the omniscience and omnipresence of God, i.e. that God sees all, knows all, and His presence is everywhere.

FANDANGO: Lively, regional Spanish dance and its music.

FRANCISCAN: Member of the Catholic religious order founded by Saint Francis of Assisi in 1209. Franciscans are dedicated to preaching, missionary work, and charitable acts.

FRESCO: A method of painting on fresh wall plaster; the design is then absorbed into the plaster as it dries and becomes a permanent part of the wall.

FRIEZE: A decorative band usually placed along the top of a wall. Stencils cut from cow hides were used by workers to create repeated patterns.

NATIVE AMERICANS: The indigenous people of the Americas. The Native Americans of Alta California lived in the area for several thousand years before the arrival of Europeans.

NAVE: The central space in a church which leads from the entrance to the altar.

NEOPHYTE: A religious convert; a newly baptized Native American.

PEDIMENT: A triangular architectural feature or decoration over a doorway or window.

PRESIDIO: Fortified military outpost or fort. The Spanish presidios in Alta California included barracks, workshops, stables, and a chapel.

QUADRANGLE: Four-sided enclosure. Most missions were laid out using a quadrangle design.

PULPIT: Raised platform in a church used for preaching. The sounding board or canopy over the pulpit is called the *tornavoz* in Spanish.

PUEBLO: The non-Native American towns established to help colonize Alta California.

REFECTORY: The dining area in a mission.

SANCTUARY: Part of the church containing the altar.

SCONCE: A hanging or wall-mounted candle holder, usually with a mirror to reflect the light. Missions made their own candles from cattle tallow.

SECULARIZATION: The process under which the Mexican government removed the mission lands from the jurisdiction of the Franciscans (who were replaced by secular priests). Half the mission land, theoretically, was turned over to the Native Americans.

TILE ROOF: Made of clay tiles (Sp. *tejas*) shaped over log molds (not over Native American women's thighs as legend has it). The tiles were then fired in a kiln which made them hard and, most importantly, weatherproof.

TRANSEPT: That part of a cruciform church that crosses at right angles between the nave and the apse.

VAQUERO: Cowboy, cattle hand.

VIGAS: Ceiling beams or rafters made from single logs or poles to support the ceiling and roof. The width of a church or room.

Bibliography

Hagemon, Fred. *California's Mission La Purisima Conception* (Santa Barbara Trust for Historic Preservation, 1991).

Hannaford Donald. *Spanish-Colonial or Adobe Architecture of California* (Architectural Book Publishing, 1931).

Historic American Building Survey (HABS, Library of Congress, Mission Archives, online, 1933).

Johnson, Paul et al. *The California Missions* (Lane Publishing: Menlo Park, CA, 1979).

Kimbro, Edna & Julia Costelo. *The California Missions* (The Getty Conservation Institute: Los Angeles, CA, 2009).

McCumsey, Robert. *California Missions Measured Drawings, Historic American Building Survey*. (Learning Windows: Santa Margarita, CA, 1999).

McLaughlin, David. *The California Missions Source Book* (Pentacle Press: Palo Alto, CA, 2009).

Newcomb, Rexford. *The Old Mission Churches and Historic Houses of California: Their History, Architecture, Art and Lore* (J.B. Lippincott Co.: New York, NY, 1925).

Ruscin, Terry. *Mission Memoirs: A Collection of Photographs, Sketches & Reflections of California's Past* (Sunbelt Publications: San Diego CA, 1999).

Sewall, Jock M. *Mediterranean Architecture: A Sourcebook of Architectural Elements* (Schiffer Publishing: Atlgen, PA, 2011).

The Spanish West (Time Life Education, 1976).

Staats, H. Phillip. *California Architecture in Santa Barbara* (Architectural Book Publishing, 1929).

Stern, Jean. *Romance of the Bells: The California Missions in Art* (The Irvine Museum, 1995).

Toomey, Donald. *The Spell of California's Spanish Colonial Missions* (Sunstone Press: Santa Fe, NM, 2001).

Wakely, David. *A Sense of Mission: Historic Churches of the Southwest* (Chronicle Books: San Francisco, CA, 1994).

Online Resources for Further Study

History

California Mission Foundation
www.californiamissionsfoundation.org

California Missions Resource Center
www.missionscalifornia.com

Art

Paintings of Edward Vischer:
Claremont College
http://libraries.claremont.edu/sc/collections/vischer.html

Paintings of Oriana Day:
DeYoung Museum
http://deyoung.famsf.org/search-collections

Borein and Edwin Deakin Paintings:
Mission Santa Barbara series collection housed at Santa Barbara Mission archives

Henry Chapman Ford Drawings:
USC Digital Library
http://digitallibrary.usc.edu/search

Photography of Carleton E. Watkins:
www.oac.cdlib.org/findaid/ark:13030/tf5q2nb80s

Digital Archives

As-built Measured Drawings of Missions:
HABS, Library of Congress
www.loc.gov/pictures/item/CA0418

California History:
Calisphere, University of California Bancroft Library
www.calisphere.universityofcalifornia.edu

Acknowledgments

I am deeply indebted to the digital libraries of the Internet, along with digital photography itself, which has made this book possible. Chief among the sources is Calisphere, the University of California's digital library website, and curator Susan Snyder, in particular, for the Bancroft Library for historic photographs and paintings done in the Mission era. Second in chief is the Library of Congress with its Historical American Building Survey, which in the 1930s measured the missions and put the source drawings in the public domain. Such generosity of this scope at this high level is rare.

I would like to thank The California Missions Foundation, and in particular Ruben Mendoza and Knox Mellon, its director, for sparking the idea and tracking this book's progress, along with providing knowledgeable insight on the history and evolution of the mission style. Equally important has been Dr. Mendozas help with his editorial contributions and the preparation of the Foreword to this volume. In addition, I thank Jennifer A. Lucido of CSU Monterey Bay for assisting him with the thorough transcript revisions.

I greatly appreciated the useful website Mission.com, Classbrain, and Wikipedia Commons for their short histories of the missions, and also their broad library of sources and links, which has made my work much easier. Sources are known and images have been licensed as necessary from: Public Domain Wikipedia Commons, 123RF, Shutterstock, and Bancroft Library.

Professor Warren Hawkins was like a friendly ghost through the process of getting this done, along with Schiffer Publishing, providing dependable cooperation with integrity.

Index